What People Are Saying About *Life as Play*

"Mark is a real Taoist master. In this book he shares some of the most fascinating contemporary lives of spirit you will ever read about. He has something to teach us all about living life in a spontaneous, lyrical, and non-intentional way."

—ALLAN COMBS
author of *Synchronicity, The Radiance of Being,*
and *Consciousness Explained Better*

"This book will have you throw away all your preconceived notions about spirituality. So beware, be very aware – this book may change your life."

—BONNITTA ROY
Associate Editor, *Integral Review Journal*

"Filled with wild, weird, and wonderful accounts of his interactions with numerous spiritual teachers, along with helpful summations of Taoist perspectives on feng shui, the energy body, sexual practices (and more!), My Life as Play is spiced with countless irreverent asides as well as pithy encapsulations of the wisdom of the ages: I agree almost completely with the old humbug, so he must be onto something!"

—G. WILLIAM BARNARD
Professor of Religious Studies, Southern Methodist University;
author of *Exploring Unseen Worlds: William James and The Philosophy of Mysticism* and *Living Consciousness: The Metaphysical Vision of Henri Bergson*

"The strength of this book resides in its down-to-earth, matter-of-fact tone. I especially appreciate the author's self-deprecating candor and his novel perspectives on the ideas and individuals associated with the Western popularization of Eastern philosophy and spirituality."
—MARK HARVEY, PhD
Professor of Psychology, University of North Carolina, Asheville

"The ultimate message is one I resonate with: if you are not having FUN on your path, whatever it is, you are an over-serious stick-in-the-mud, who, while getting your tough lessons in Earth Life, have missed the whole point of learning to be a Divinely Playful Human."
—MICHAEL WINN
Founder, Healing Tao USA

"This earnest, compassionate, knowledgeable, authentic, and often very funny seeker and guide, shares his odyssey of spirituality meeting the West. Yet, whatever the road, the purpose is the same: the truth is simple and playful, and as profound as anything. As his Daoist teacher put it, *This spiritual path is NOT about freeing yourself from suffering and securing your own happiness. It is about participating in something far greater.*"
—RUTH RICHARDS, MD, PhD
Professor of Psychology (consciousness and spirituality), Saybrook University; Psychiatry Lecturer, Harvard Medical School

Life As Play

Live compassionately,
intuitively, spontaneously,
and miracles will happen!

Mark J Johnson

☦
Dao Publishing
Santa Rosa, California

© Copyright 2021 by Mark J. Johnson. All rights reserved.

No part of this book may be reproduced or transmitted in any form or by any means, electronic or mechanical, including photocopying, recording, or by any information storage and retrieval system, without permission in writing from the publisher.

2021 Full Color Edition — paperback
ISBN: 978-0-9837586-9-3

2021 Full Color Edition — ebook
ISBN: 978-0-9837586-7-9

2021 Black & White Edition — paperback
ISBN: 978-0-9837586-6-2

Library of Congress Control Number: 2020924024

All images were taken by the author or Rebecca Kali or are in the public domain with the exception of the following:

© Golasza | Dreamstime.com | Buildings in Taos, last stop before entering Taos

© Sgc | Dreamstime.com | Bridge Over Rio Grande

Dao Publishing
801 Tupper Street, #1111
Santa Rosa, CA 95404

daopublishing.com
info@daopublishing.com

Why haven't you discovered your innate divinity yet?

Foreword

Mark has something to teach us about living life in a spontaneous, lyrical, and non-intentional way.

This book is told exactly the way he tells these stories in person – with a self-effacing sense of humor. His Daoist master scrubbed him clean and gouged out all his melodramatic emotions, resentments, insecurities, and non-acceptance of himself and others. Rather than treat him kindly, his master did all he could to push Mark's buttons, leaving him free of reactivity and fully able to enjoy his life as Play.

Beyond all that, Mark is a poster child for American spirituality in the 21st century. Jeffrey Kripal, in his remarkable book, *Esalen: America and the Religion of No Religion,* describes the rise of spirituality without religion in the United States during the second half of the 20th century with pioneers such as Ram Dass, Alan Watts, and Michael Murphy of Esalen who helped the search for understanding the place of humankind in a cosmos whose boundaries are being radically redefined almost daily by science. Their deepening awareness was enhanced by the recently discovered Eastern spirituality that reads more like psychology than theology.

Like Ram Dass, Mark's spiritual journey began in the eastern United States and led him eventually to the Orient, where he met his principal Daoist master and teacher. During his early years in the United States, Mark met many significant spiritual teachers whom he describes in colorful and intriguing detail. But it was in the Orient that he, like so many of his generation, found his richest spiritual inspiration.

While Ram Dass and Michael Murphy both grew up in surroundings of wealth and attended Ivy League universities, Mark is the product of a small Pennsylvania coal-mining town. He briefly attended Penn State University and completed his formal education at the Art Institute of Pittsburgh. His view of life is both artistic and practical but not necessarily literary or deeply philosophical. He is well-suited to the no-nonsense, down-to-earth attitude of Daoism. Indeed, he is a living representative of life as Play. His warmth and goodwill, along with his humor and intuitive intelligence, radiate through these pages as they radiate in his life. He is nothing less than a living embodiment of the ineffable at Play.

— Allan Combs, author of *Synchronicity,*
The Radiance of Being, and
Consciousness Explained Better

Contents

Foreword   v

Introduction   1

The Cosmos at Play   7

Playing within a Secure Family   11

Playing at College and the Art Institute   15

Playing in New York   17

My Epiphany, and Then the Miracles   19

Amazing Miracles Led to My First Spiritual Teachers   23

Learning to Play at the Vedanta Center   27

Learning to Play with Malcolm   33

Learning to Play with Earnly   41

Learning to Play with Other Teachers   51

Learning to Play at the Tassajara Zen Center   55

Playing with Daoists in Colorado   59

Playing at the Taoist Sanctuary in Los Angeles   63

Messiah of the Modern Age?   71

Meeting My Teacher / Dragon in Taiwan   75

Editing with My Daoist Teacher   85

Dragon's Play in Taiwan   89

The Dragon Comes to Malibu	93
Playing in Malibu	99
Learning While Teaching	107
Teaching Popular Feng Shui	111
Teaching Natural Feng Shui	115
The Nine Daoist Vortices	123
Teaching Daoist Sexual Cultivation	133
Playing While Thinking	139
Playing with Famous People	153
From Heaven to Purgatory Again	159
Marital Bliss, Divorce, And "Graduation"	163
Playing in Retirement	171
Playing in China and Tibet	177
The Biggest Challenges Facing Humanity	181
Playing with Death and Immortality	195
Playing with Reincarnation	203
Playing with Enlightenment	209
Life and the Universe at Play	217
Epilogue	221
About the Author	225

Introduction

The great oneness at the core of our being is Playful, and a Playful life is a joyful life.

In these pages, you will discover how to allow your innate Playful essence to express itself in every moment. Think of my story as a tour and initiation into a life of Play. This book is filled with tales of the unexpected and the unique circumstances that characterize a life of Play. This is not a book about playing. It is a Playful book.

The kind of Play I refer to (Play with a capital "P") is certainly not the play of the idle rich, nor is it limited to throwing a Frisbee around on a summer day. A child is incapable of the kind of Play I describe, for children know nothing of time or consequences. There is a big difference between the Play of a sage and that of a two-year-old – it is the difference between being childlike and childish.

The kind of Play I encourage can only be expressed by a mature adult who can appreciate and embody the Playfulness of the Universe in its many expressions of synchronicities, paradox, humor, and being "in the zone." More importantly, if there is an absence of the creativity, spontaneity, curiosity, and mystery that generate these qualities (and generates the Universe), there is no real Play, in my opinion. I emphasize those four aspects of Play in particular because they are most often absent in people trying to be spiritual or trying to appear spiritual to themselves and others.

Mystery is especially important. The Universe and beyond is an incredible mystery, so how can anyone claiming to be "one with everything" have no sense of mystery about them?

Are the qualities of creativity, spontaneity, curiosity, and mystery present in your life?

When they exist in your life, you will find that filling out your income tax can be Playful. You can relax and Play with paradox, confusion, and chaos. You can even accept pain and death without losing your sense of lightness and wholeness. This is not to say that life always flows effortlessly for people who can truly Play. They have challenges just like everyone else, except they are not as bothered by adverse circumstances because they are not so strongly attached to their egos. The size of your ego is not the problem. What's important is how strongly you are attached to it, whatever its size.

My experience tells me it is often more difficult to transcend a small, self-restricted life rather than one that is more open, expansive, and willing to evolve.

Regardless of what is happening in your life, it can be Play even when you are being challenged.

Play is also a perspective, and perspectives create our world. Centuries ago, an eclipse of the sun would cause mass panic. Today, people go out of their way to view them – same phenomena, different perspectives, different reactions. Imagine how our lives would be enhanced if we were in a constant state of Play. Take a moment and think about what YOUR life would be like if you played at it more and worked at it less?

My scientific friends assure me that healthy growth and creativity most easily happen when one is playing. They point out how many of the great and creative companies around the world now have game-playing stations and even quiet rooms for meditation. They insist that playing is a fundamental survival instinct and a necessary ingredient in maintaining the neuroplasticity of our brains.

Play also partakes of the instant-by-instant delight of pure being. A Playful person can be dancing one minute, then sitting quietly the next – and both expressions can be Playful. This level of Play mostly occurs when we recognize we are participating in the co-creation of the Universe. In that state, every action becomes an effortless, natural response to circumstances. Within that state, there arises the realization that everyone and everything IS oneself and that everything one does is done TO oneself. When that realization becomes an abiding state, we express ourselves from the depths of our being.

That all-encompassing state of identity with the Other is the origin and foundation of love, compassion, and Play.

The connection between Play and the Oneness occurred to me as I was reading the 2,000 year-old-Hindu epic, "The Mahabharata." That poem refers to the manifest world as the "Lila" or Play of the great Oneness and asserts that we, in our essence, are the great Oneness and are therefore Playful. If the core of our being is Oneness, and if the great Oneness is constantly creating and changing spontaneously, then why aren't we? It was then that I realized this world is not a cosmic mistake, nor a veil of tears to be endured and transcended as quickly as possible.

It is an endless Playground to be enjoyed.

Thanks to a life-changing experience in my early twenties, I set out to find others who embodied this idea and could teach me how to also live Playfully. To my surprise, most of the spiritual people I encountered were just busily trying to "feel good" all the time. However, there were always a precious few who seemed to exhibit those Playful skills I was looking for – and it is my pleasure to introduce you to the ones I have known. Finding and living with people who manifest divine qualities was always a priority for me, and this book is filled with the lessons I learned from each of them. Seeking the counsel and friendship of wise and loving souls is a great way to live.

To read about the lives of the Buddha, Lao Tzu, Moses, Jesus, Muhammad, Zoroaster, Ramakrishna, the Holy Mother, Ramana Maharshi, and Gandhi (to name only a few of my favorites) is inspiring in itself, but to have lived with some of those kinds of people and cultivated oneself under their tutelage is quite another matter.

How would you feel if you had lived in Jerusalem at the time of Jesus and never met the guy? What a tragedy it would have been to have known the Buddha personally, but due to religious prejudice or tunnel vision, you remained closed to his message of compassion.

Although I was born into a middle-class family in a small coal-mining town in central Pennsylvania, I was later fortunate to have met many of the great spiritual teachers of the second half of the 20th century. However, I spent the majority of my time with Vedantists, Zen teachers, and Daoist (Taoist) masters. (Note that I have chosen this spelling of Daoism instead of the more familiar Taoism because it is phonetically correct.)

My mentors are the treasures of my life, for it was they who showed me how to Play. My present, Playful life was nurtured by their attention, endless patience, and a lot of love over a long period of time. Everything of value in this book comes through them.

Within these pages, you will share in my first epiphany in New York City in 1963, which led to my first spiritual teachers in a Florida ashram. I stayed with them for ten years until I moved to California to find some Daoists. Unfortunately for me, I got enamored with a famous Buddhist master in Tassajara, California, who died within a year! So I went back to my old ashram in Florida. I stayed there for two more years. However, the insistent call of Daoism led me to a Daoist Center in Los Angeles, where I stayed for three years!

All that pales in comparison to my 20-plus years of intense self-cultivation in the 1970s, '80s, and '90s under the tutelage of a powerful Chinese Daoist master – who prefers to remain anonymous. That era includes my studying with him in Taiwan in 1974 and the remarkable circumstances that surrounded his coming to the United States a year later.

He eventually arrived in the "wild and dangerous" hills of Malibu, where we established a center and acupuncture clinic for him. For eight years, I studied Tai Ji (Tai Chi), Chi Gung, acupuncture, Daoist exorcism, spiritual sexual practices, and how to integrate our three bodies: the physical, the bioelectrical (acupuncture meridians), and our auric body. That period was followed by an assignment to teach all over the country, which I did for another 15 years.

One of my first assignments involved my going to Tulsa, Oklahoma in 1982 to teach Tai Ji to Frances Ford Coppola and all the now famous "megastars" who were with him at the making of the movie *The Outsiders*. That movie launched the careers of Nicolas Cage, Tom Cruise, Diane Lane, Patrick Swayze, Matt Dillon, and Ralph Macchio. I stayed for the making of another movie, *Rumble Fish*, and got to know the young Mickey Rourke and Dennis Hopper. When I eventually realized they were all more interested in making movies than the precious gift I had to offer, I left the "show biz" people.

I went to Taos, New Mexico to enjoy an early retirement at age 40, but after a mere three years, my teacher gave me another "heavenly assignment" (as he called them) to go to New York City again. No epiphany this time. I got into some really weird stuff – like marriage and raising a family!

I evolved spiritually much faster because of that assignment than from all previous mystical training and teaching. After a seven-year marriage, we divorced, and I really did semi-retire to Northern California where I get my transcendence through ultralight flying and astronomy, which are much safer than marriage.

This book also includes chapters on integral thinking; the fun and difficulty of translating Chinese; Feng Shui; sensing our auric bodies; death and immortality; reincarnation; and enlightenment. One chapter focuses on how we are doomed if we do not get in touch with and integrate our subconscious. Pay close attention to that one. This book ends with the nine precepts of Play.

The most consistent theme throughout this book is that of the power of synchronicities to encourage a life of Play and how it reveals the interconnectedness of all creation. So if an ordinary person like myself can Play in every instant, then you surely can too.

I hope you will recognize this Playful place within yourself and allow it to expand. To the extent my life has gone beyond the norm, may it inspire you to take the plunge into the unknown in your own life. And now, join the cosmic jester and universal trickster as I meander my way through a life of Play. Let the mystery, magic, and miracles begin!

Mark Johnson
Autumn 2020

The Cosmos at Play

This is a book about Play as a practice because "Play" is the nature of the Universe. When we play "with" the Universe – as opposed to against it, which we humans do so often, as we insist our little egos know better than the All-That-Is – we find ourselves in synchronicity and flow.

Before getting into the power and availability of synchronicities, I want to set the stage for how and why they exist. Since I do not want to get ahead of myself, I will first mention the Universe's role in it all and then how synchronicities first began manifesting in my early life.

So let's start at the beginning…and I do mean THE BEGINNING because I remember it like it was yesterday…

Everything was dark because the present Universe had not yet been created. And then, all of a sudden – BANG – Everything got started from Nothing. Around 13.8 billion years ago, our present Universe was reborn from the unimaginable heat and pressure of the "Big Crunch" of the previous Universe. This is the current theory I subscribe to because it implies that this Universe has been re-birthing itself forever, which makes it eternal just as we are.

Then about 4.6 billion years ago, our sun and solar system were created with the material ejected from the dying stars that surrounded them. Our sun is an average-sized star and is a solitary traveler around the Milky Way, which puts it in a minority class because most of the stars travel with a companion star. In other words, we are on an ordinary planet circling a single sun without a companion.

Our planet has given birth to life that evolved from simple organisms to extremely complex ones, to the point where one of the more complex species (humans) now has the capacity to destroy itself and most life on the planet. How's that for cosmic irony? Never mind all that. Those billions of years of evolution were merely leading to…all of us!

Which brings me to my own birth because it is still fresh in my mind. I was born on a dark and stormy morning in the midst of the most destructive war this planet has known. Under intense contraction and pressure (similar to our Universe just before the Big Bang), I was born into a small coal-mining town in central Pennsylvania on October 20, 1942. I was the first of four children born to a dispassionate, agnostic, workaholic Republican father and a highly emotional, devout Roman Catholic, Democrat mother. My mother was part German, and my father came from a family of pacifist Quakers. This might explain why I spent a great deal of my youth starting fights and then refusing to participate in them. Is it any wonder I ended up a highly emotional, dispassionate, lazy workaholic?

Why someone who was to become a mystical Daoist would be born into a Roman Catholic family in Pennsylvania to a coal-mining superintendent and a nurse is difficult to explain. I am just grateful it happened that way because they created an environment that supported my needs at the time. Perhaps "the powers that be" provided the perfect "culture dish" for me to help bring Eastern philosophy to the West – or maybe they just had a good sense of humor.

However, from my perspective, I felt like the canary in the coal mine. Would I survive being dropped into the dark pit of ignorance and superstition that was central Pennsylvania in those days? Considering my attitude at the time, it is understandable why I fled that area the night I graduated from high school and seldom went back. On the other hand, my present-day Pennsylvania friends who knew me then insist my condescension toward the town and its people results from my delusion of adequacy!

I don't want to disparage the area too severely since my first mystical experiences happened there. The word mystical has nothing to do with psychic phenomena or the occult, by the way. By mystical experiences, I mean knowing the Great Oneness directly. Since those early experiences transcended my life and even the Universe itself, I will include them in this chapter because they became the foundation for my lifelong spiritual quest.

I have heard that many children have those kinds of early life experiences, so my stories may seem familiar. The following incidents, and all the other personal anecdotes I will share with you throughout this book, are either examples of my life as Play or significant experiences that led to that state of being – which by the way, is open and accessible to everyone.

I remember telling my mother when I was in my crib at age three that everything would start to get small just before I fell asleep. It was similar to looking through the wrong end of a pair of binoculars. While playing with my soft, white, fuzzy "blankie" and lying next to my younger brother, who shared my bed for over ten years, I experienced myself as a huge, still presence that seemed to be witnessing everything and WAS everything at the same time. It was quite peaceful, and the enormity of it was breathtaking.

I mostly experienced that sense of being everything whenever my brother stirred next to me. I felt it was me stirring. However, what started as a personal experience quickly became a non-experience because my sense of identity dissolved until there was only a vague awareness of rapid expansion leading to eventual stillness until I woke up the next morning.

Those mystical experiences came and went over a period of several years. My mother assured me it was only eyestrain and advised me to rub my eyes to make it go away. Sure enough, I stopped having them after a lot of eye rubbing. Makes you wonder how many other mystical experiences children have that are "rubbed out" by parents who cannot see beyond the ordinary.

Certain other of my strong traits started expressing themselves around that time. One was my not liking to be confined in any way – physically, intellectually, or spiritually. My parents often said there was not a playpen I could not break out of. Once in my early teens, I was caught reading about Eastern religions and got hell for it, and around age 15, I started a rocket program to break the confines of gravity. And at age 17, I went so far as to play God by creating a three-minute, 30,000 still-framed animated dinosaur movie by putting life into clay objects – and I intend to continue playing God until I get it right.

Playing within a Secure Family

Many people evolve their spiritual lives precisely because of their unstable home life. However, if you have a choice, incarnate into a secure and loving family next time. I will never forget what my uncle used to tell me: "Mark, if you have a choice between being rich and happy, or poor and miserable, choose the former." How could I go wrong with advice like that? My father gave me the freedom to be myself, and my mother provided the love and stability of our home. That combination provided the deep sense of security and fearlessness I always seemed to have, which allowed me to explore so many of life's possibilities.

My fondest memories of my dad were when he drove us every weekend to the mines he supervised. I still recall the pungent smell of the carbonate lamps we attached to our hard hats. Deep underground, it was so quiet I could hear the blood swishing through my veins – which turned out to be my first experience of the great silence that would revisit me throughout my life.

My most profound takeaway from our weekly visits to the dark, silent depths was a willingness and comfortableness to probe darkness later in life. Those experiences led to my integrating my shadow at an early age. To this day, I continue plumbing the depths of my subconscious and unconscious. I recognize this exploration as central to understanding myself and see it as a portal to integrating my entire being.

To the degree that you integrate the energies of your darkest fears, anger, and despair will you experience the heights of spiritual awareness.

In contrast to my father, my mother was constantly interacting with us. She was the disciplinarian and center of our family. She swore like a trooper and never saw the irony in calling me an S.O.B. Her favorite expression was, "Just wait until your father gets home!" She never knew we feared her a lot more than we feared him. My mother was devoted to Holy Mother the Church and doing crossword puzzles. She made sure we got to mass every Sunday, whether we wanted to or not, and pushed us all to become altar boys. She is probably in heaven right now, lighting candles for my return to the church.

My warmest memories of her involved the times I was sick or trying to fake an illness. She fussed over me with special foods, stories, and temperature readings. It is a wonder I wasn't sick all the time just to get more of that kind of attention. Unfortunately for me, she was such a good nurse that I was never able to trick her into letting me stay home from school. When she left my bedroom, I used to take the thermometer out from under my tongue and hold it next to a light bulb to run up the temperature to a convincing level for the illness I was trying to fake. I suppose that 112° Fahrenheit was a bit excessive because she never fell for any of my shenanigans. She was smarter than my dad, but she hid it well.

What a study in contrasts they were! My father was a refined, gentle, aloof intellectual with enormous integrity. He lived with a quick-tempered woman, who was all heart underneath her rough exterior. They were the perfect example of opposites attracting each other to achieve balance.

Their marriage seemed to work in spite of their many differences. I seldom heard them raise their voices to each other or strongly disagree about anything, even though they lived in two different worlds.

My first brother was born on my first birthday. Our third brother arrived five years later, and our sister was born 12 years after me. I didn't know her very well because she was only five when I went off to college. Every night at 6 o'clock, my father arrived at the door with his black-metal lunch pail in hand. My mother always waited in the doorway to kiss him. Then, as a family, we headed to the dinner table. That pattern continued unchanged for nearly 17 years. The security that comes with a daily ritual like that is priceless and can open up all kinds of new possibilities – as you will see in my life, and most importantly, in the lives of the extraordinary teachers I have met.

Playing at College and the Art Institute

I left the security of our home to go to college, and sometimes I wish I had stayed home. In high school, I managed a B average even though I was always outside blowing up rockets or in the basement trying to remember whether that clay dinosaur's tail was swishing to the right or the left. In college, that work ethic earned me F's. In addition to having no study skills, I discovered women (in the Biblical sense) my first week at Penn State and spent most of my time making up for lost time. I also left the Catholic Church then, for who needs God when one is having sex regularly? I could even eat hamburgers on Fridays! (Eating meat on Fridays was considered a mortal sin in those days.) My motto was, "Thank God, I'm an atheist." After one semester of nonstop sex and Friday beef-eating, I was on academic probation and decided I had to find something else to do.

In late December 1960, I quit my study of aeronautical engineering and got a job waiting tables in Atlantic City during the Christmas break. While cruising the boardwalk one sunny day, I discovered I had a talent for art. As I stopped to watch a portrait artist, an overpowering feeling came over me that I could draw as well as he did. I went back to my motel room and decided to give it a try. To my surprise, my portraits were quite life-like. As a result, I spent that winter doing portraits for money. Imagine having no artistic inclination for 17 years then discovering your artistic talent!

Drawing seemed like a fun and effortless way to make a living. I enrolled in the Art Institute of Pittsburgh and promised my father I wouldn't waste his money as I had done at Penn State. For the next two-and-a-half years, I lived in a big house with four other artists – a life that could best be described as an endless beer party.

Between seducing the ladies with portraits and spending weekends at rock concerts, I managed to squeeze in just enough artwork to keep my father and my teachers happy. This carefree, almost idyllic life ended with my seeking my fortune in the Big Apple. That move alone changed my perspective about life.

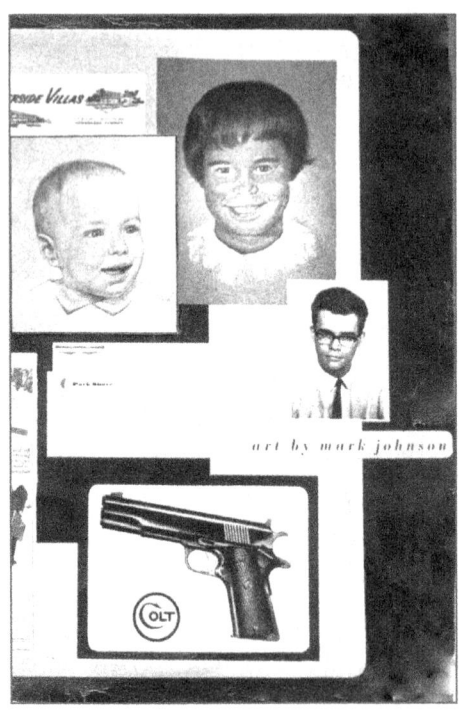

A showing of my Art Institute assignments at graduation.

Playing in New York

I chose New York for two reasons. First, I felt that New York City was the only town large enough to appreciate my talents (ha-ha), and second, I had an uncle who lived in Brooklyn Heights who was willing to take me in. Every night I sat in his small apartment and listened to him and his Columbia University PhD friends drinking themselves into incoherence while discussing "the great issues of life."

During the day, I apprenticed at a large advertising agency where the director had frequent bouts of hitting his forehead due to job stress. After watching him being carried out of the agency on a stretcher one fine day and observing the meaningless lives of my uncle and his friends, I realized that playing was not the foundation of everyone's life. That was quite a shock to such a naive young man, spoiled by an effortless life and never knowing anything but fun.

While trying to make sense of all the pain and pain avoidance I saw around me, my new awareness was intensified by my uncle encouraging me to read Dostoevsky, Sartre, Nietzsche, Camus, Kierkegaard, and other Existentialists. Unfortunately, they mostly said that life is inherently absurd, and we need to bring our own meaning to it. (And the only meaning they brought to it was "Life is absurd.") The more I read their books, the more I concluded that the only authentic thing to do to resolve this absurdity was to commit honorable suicide. I did the next best thing to killing myself – I moved to Queens, which was oh-so-boring in those days.

I compensated by hanging out in Greenwich Village chess houses until the wee hours. Even the chess houses could not compensate for all the pain and stress I saw on the faces of most people in New York. It was all getting to me. I had not been exposed to such levels of pain before, and it saddened me to my core. I characterized those few months in New York as "the agony and the agony," leading to my epiphany and my first spiritual teachers.

My Epiphany,
and Then the Miracles

It was in New York, the place where I experienced such agony and angst, where I had the epiphany that would set the course for my life.

How do I describe this life-changing experience? I could say it was a dream, except that dreams do not precipitate a complete reversal of a life's direction. Nor do they impact with such an energy that knocks a person out of bed and lasts for several days. I swear I was semi-conscious when it was happening, and I was not my old self for two days afterward.

My "non-ordinary" experience started with a huge black bear chasing me through a dark forest, and it was so real I could feel his breath on the back of my neck the closer he got. All of a sudden, a shining staircase appeared in front of me, and I ran up it as fast as I could – thinking that fat bear could never navigate that spiral staircase. It just shows you how wrong I can be sometimes.

As I reached the top of the staircase, I braced to kick him in the head. It was then that I saw his face for the first time – it was the face of a Teddy bear! Such a loving and gentle face I had never seen on any creature before. As we got eyeball to eyeball, he reached out to me and said, "Why are you running from me? I am you!" He then hugged me with an energy that felt like a tsunami of love that left me in an altered state for days.

Over the years, I related the experience to three or four psychiatrist friends, and they all came to roughly the same conclusion. My subconscious integrated with my conscious mind, and when that happens, a person's energy field is far greater than when they are separated. The power of that experience could explain why I have not altered my life's direction or urgent message to humanity since then. Which is: "If we as a species do not integrate with our subconscious to allow for higher spiritual evolution, we are all doomed." (More details on this important subject in the later chapters).

Three days later, I came back to "normal" but with thoughts and energies I did not know existed. Those new energies and insights immediately elicited the first original thoughts of my life and the profound changes that happened within hours.

And soon after that, this lofty epiphany had its first impact on my mundane life. Standing in front of my bathroom mirror shaving at 6 a.m. on one of the coldest mornings that Queens, New York had experienced in a long time, I suddenly realized I hated having to shave. I also hated 6 o'clock in the morning, cold weather, and New York City. Suddenly, I froze with the horror of it all. So I said to myself, "I don't like getting up early, and I don't like New York, nor my job, or any of the friends I have made so far. So what am I doing here? I am free to do anything I want – and by the way, what the hell DO I want?"

I decided right then and there I wanted to live like Gauguin in Tahiti – eating fruit off the trees, having sex with the natives, and painting all day (but not necessarily in that order). That seemed like perpetual bliss, so what was stopping me? Nothing. I put down the razor and called the advertising agency and said, "I want my final paycheck."

With money in hand, I headed off to the docks in New York to work my way to Tahiti on a freighter. The dockworkers patiently explained that freighters don't go to Tahiti from New York though I could leave from the West Coast. The next thing I knew, I was hitchhiking down the New Jersey turnpike with $40 in my pocket, headed roughly in the direction of Tahiti. My life of "playing at life" was over, and my learning how to "Play with life" was just beginning.

Amazing Miracles Led to My First Spiritual Teachers

Since I hated cold weather, I decided to visit an artist friend living in Miami for the winter. I figured I would then work my way to Los Angeles doing odd jobs and from there, planned to take a freighter straight to Tahiti. That was the extent of my master plan. I trusted the Universe would continue providing for me – and it did.

Out there all alone on the New Jersey Turnpike with my thumb out on my 21st birthday, I was picked up almost immediately by an elderly couple in an old Plymouth going to St. Petersburg, Florida. After a few minutes of introductions, I discovered they were from my hometown in central Pennsylvania! And not only that, the man said he had worked for my father for 40 years! He said my father was the finest man he ever met. They told me I was like the son they never had, and suddenly I had free transportation, meals, and lodging all the way to Florida.

What are the chances of that happening? Meaningful coincidences called "synchronicities" are one of the most overlooked phenomena we humans experience. I have observed that most people do not even know they exist, and more importantly, how to elicit them when needed.

Sometimes people confuse synchronicities with coincidences because they both involve incidents "coinciding" (happening at the same time). The difference is synchronicities have a greater meaning and often seem "arranged" by some mysterious force. For example, we have all had the experience of thinking of a person – usually someone quite familiar – and then a few minutes later, they call. That could be considered a coincidence. Contrast that with my being picked up by a couple from my hometown, who knew my dad and respected him so much that they virtually adopted me.

Or contrast that with another experience I had while driving through North Carolina on my way home for Christmas one year. Being young and footloose, I had only $10 in spare cash with me. I was driving a Renault, a fairly rare car in those days, and stopped to pick up a hitchhiker, figuring I could have him drive while I slept so we could make better time. I was sleeping in the back seat when I heard a crash. I awoke to find the engine had come loose from its moorings and had literally fallen out the bottom of the car. The hitchhiker and I found a board nearby, and we levered the engine back into place – but the car was not drivable. We were right near an exit, so the two of us pushed the car off onto a downward spiraling off-ramp. When we got to the bottom, we looked up – and right there was a Renault dealer. The dealer bolted the engine in and charged me ... $10, the exact amount I had in my pocket! As we were leaving, he said, "You know we're the only Renault dealer in North Carolina."

Far too meaningful to be a mere coincidence!

Even that synchronicity is considered kindergarten stuff compared to the synchronicities I experienced after studying with some of the powerful teachers I met and cultivating the practices they taught. For now, I only want to say that if you stay open and empty and allow your innate divinity to flow thru you, and especially if you are on this Earth to help others and all creatures, you will have synchronicities beyond what you can imagine, and always there when you need them. I will later reveal many synchronistic incidences, including the mind-boggling story of what happened to my favorite Daoist teacher when he came to America.

Through synchronicities, Nature demonstrates the underlying unity and timeless interconnectedness of life.

While traveling the Eastern seaboard with my adopted family, I asked if I could visit the Extra Sensory Perception lab at Duke University in North Carolina. I had always been interested in psychic phenomena, and I did not want to miss the opportunity.

As synchronicity would have it, Dr. J. B. Rhine and Dr. William Roll were standing on the front steps of the psychology building talking when we arrived. They were two of the most famous researchers in parapsychology at that time. To my surprise, they invited me in to be tested.

Dr. Roll asked me to guess what card was coming up next in the sequence, along with several other tests that were variations on the same theme. I scored very low on a possible 100 correct guesses, but he got excited because he said I had to be psychic to be that bad! However, he seemed more interested in my skeptical nature than my psychic abilities. He again surprised me by asking me to interview 15 psychics in the Tampa/St. Petersburg area when I got down there to see if any of them warranted further investigation.

As I worked through that list in Florida, I was thrown out of a lot of séances and psychic workshops. Most of what I saw could be explained by means other than having psychic abilities, and a few of them were downright fraudulent. One time, in a darkened room, a psychic drew our attention to a dim, red light above us, which he claimed was a descended master. When the lights came on, I found a small red light bulb embedded in the ceiling. Concerned that I would expose his trick, he quickly gave me my money back and whisked me out the door. During another séance, one old spirit claimed he had lived on the Earth 40,000 years ago and blabbered incessantly about nothing for an hour. I remember thinking, what in hell am I going to learn from a person who lived 40,000 years ago except maybe a few good recipes for mastodon burgers?

It is no wonder psychic phenomena have such a bad reputation. As to those who believed everything they saw and heard, where was their discretion? I recommended only two psychics from the list Dr. Roll gave me. In spite of the disappointing results, those investigations were valuable because they led me to my first spiritual teachers.

In the course of interviewing the psychics, I asked each of them who they thought was the most talented psychic in the area. All inquiries led me to the Reverend Malcolm McBride Panton. He was not only a famous psychic, he was the head of The Advaita Vedanta Center, which meant nothing to me at the time. However, that center was to become my home for the next ten years.

Learning to Play at the Vedanta Center

On a dark and humid night in late 1963, I first met the Reverend Malcolm McBride Panton and his wife, Earnly. They greeted me at the door of their little center in St. Petersburg, Florida, and asked, "Where have you come from? Where are you going? And how do you make your living?"

I replied, "I have come from New York on my way to Tahiti to become a beachcomber. I am presently selling vacuum cleaners."

Malcolm said, "If you don't find Tahiti within yourself, the trip will be a waste of your time." As for my job, he suggested I give up all my "attachments." The truth and humor of that statement stopped me in my tracks, and the direction of my life changed instantly. After securing a job in graphic design, I no longer needed to worry about my "attachments." I enrolled in all their classes and took up residence a few houses away as the first step toward finding my Tahiti within, whatever that meant. Apparently, that was the first lesson I needed to absorb: Finding our inner truth is more important than chasing after some mental fantasy.

Their center in southeast St. Petersburg had the only surviving 60-foot royal palms in the city. Those magnificent trees, and a giant banyan tree across the street, imbued the area with a feeling of sanctity and nobility.

Although the building where they had their services was quite small, it had a calming energy. There was nothing inside to distract you. The stillness reminded me of my time deep in the coal mines. Unlike the coal mines, the stillness in their Vedanta center came from all the meditation everyone did there.

It was also the center of a happy community that grew up beyond the Center itself. For one thing, the Pantons held talks and Yoga classes daily in their home next to the center. We members eventually bought or rented every house around them. We were all in and out of their center daily and were constantly interacting with each other. Since our houses were close to each other, the entire block reeked of curry and Indian incense.

Since I did not know what Advaita Vedanta meant, they explained the word "Advaita" means non-duality, and the word "Vedanta" means the end or goal of the Vedas – the holy books of Hinduism. Non-duality means that an individual's essence and the Great Oneness are one and the same. I took to Vedanta like a duck to water.

At last, a religion and philosophy that made sense to me. This was not a vengeful male God with the character of a petulant child dictating from on high, exclusively through Jews and Christians. No more miserable sinners needing to be saved. No more thinly disguised cannibalistic sacraments, like ingesting the blood and flesh of a man in order to share in his divinity. No need to pour water on the heads of babies to cleanse a non-existent stain on their souls. No need to cut off the skin on their little dicks as part of some cosmic covenant. No more virginal mother stories, especially when Jesus obviously had an older brother. No more patriarchal bullshit like misrepresenting Mary Magdalene as a whore so the early church fathers could continue suppressing women. Also, I never did accept the myth that there is no salvation except through Jesus or anybody else. Don't misunderstand me – I like Jesus. I just can't stand the mythology the Christian Churches have created about him and the relentless control they continually exert.

As Swami Beyondananda, "The Wise Yogi from Muskogee," observed, "Spirituality is everyone's connection with the Divine, and religion is crowd control."

Also, to paraphrase the Swami, I believe it is time we evolved from being children of God to being adults of God.

Most important to me, I no longer had to accept a meaningless existence with no possibility of transcendence. From Vedanta, I learned that:

Your Life's goal is to realize your innate oneness with everything.

When you arrive at this knowing in Vedanta, there is no inquisition, no excommunication, just congratulations upon completion. You experience life primarily as a spiritual journey, and we have as many lifetimes as we need and want to live our spiritual nature here on Earth.

What a breath of fresh air this was! We had Hatha Yoga classes twice a week and studied the Upanishads, the Bhagavad Gita, and the writings of the Hindu philosopher Shankara, who consolidated the Advaita Vedanta doctrine in the 8th Century BCE. We also studied the teachings of the 19th Century Hindu sage Ramakrishna and my favorite sage, Ramana Maharshi, who lived in the early 20th century. Ramana developed a self-inquiry process that consists of asking the questions, "Who am I? For whom is there freedom from bondage? Who is the 'me' I am identifying with?" And then we were encouraged to be empty and open to the response that comes to us.

I practiced Ramana Maharshi's self-inquiry method for years until I experienced myself as the eternal witness, which I now recognize as what I was experiencing as a child. It is misleading to call it a state. It is more like an expanded awareness from which all things derive their being.

The only time you can abide in the now...
IS NOW!

Malcolm once told a famous story that more accurately describes the sheer magnitude of that awareness, and it went something like this:

Once there was a brash, young monkey, leader of all the monkeys in the world. His name was Monkey King (also known as Sun Wukong). One day, he came upon the Buddha sitting on his throne with many attendants surrounding him. Because Monkey was jealous, he challenged the Buddha to a race to the end of the Universe. Monkey got the Buddha to agree that if he won the race, he could sit on the Buddha's throne and have the attendants cater to his every need. Keep in mind that Monkey had extraordinary powers. He could travel over a billion miles every time he jumped, so he had every reason to be confident.

Ready, set, go! The monkey took off like a shot and, in a short time, arrived at the end of the Universe indicated by five huge pillars. He decided to prove he was there by urinating at the base of the pillars. When he returned, he saw the Buddha still sitting on his throne, so Monkey assumed he had won. The Buddha, however, just smiled and opened his fist to show Monkey's urine running down between his five fingers. The Buddha didn't have to race Monkey to the edge of the Universe because he already was there. It is like the Ocean that does not need to travel from California to Japan – it already is there!

Learning to Play with Malcolm

Malcolm was one of the more "awake" people I have known and he hadn't achieved that awareness in some ashram in India. He forged his understanding of the world as a copywriter and on the streets of New York. He was best known as an art critic for *New Yorker* magazine, and he had been a writer for the radio program "The Shadow."

I soon realized he was not just a local St. Petersburg psychic. He was known worldwide because he frequently traveled with Arthur Ford, who undoubtedly was the most recognized psychic at that time.

At one of their demonstrations, he met his future wife, Earnly. She introduced him to Vedanta and together they became disciples of Swami Nikhilananda, the founder of the Ramakrishna-Vivekananda Center of New York. Just knowing Malcolm and Earnly gained me credibility with many of the Vedanta teachers in the world.

However, more importantly for me, it was through his nurturing of my psychic abilities that I was finally able to resolve the question of whether or not communication with the spirit world is possible. Although I had seen many phonies, and was skeptical of the possibility of spirit communication, I asked Malcolm if there was anything to it. He responded, "You can go to every psychic in the country and never know for sure. What you need to do is develop it yourself. Then you will be convinced."

He surprised me by starting a Wednesday night psychic development class. About ten of us would go into a dark room and practice receiving messages from the so-called spirit world. He was always with us. His gentle influence and energies nurtured our progress.

I don't mean to imply we all became famous psychics. However, after a few years of practice, a few of us got pretty good at clairvoyance or seeing and describing people's dead friends and giving specific details about their lives when they were on the Earth plane. All the while, I was unsure about the source of our information.

I suspected we were merely tuning into each other's memories. In other words, we were picking each other's brains. The details we were able to glean were impressive in themselves, but I was more interested in the possibility of spirit communication than in demonstrating mental telepathy. Communication from the spirit world could only be proven with information that nobody in the class knew. It finally came to me from the dead brother of a friend of mine from high school.

One night, a woman in our class said, "A man named Ollie is coming to Mark." I said, "I know a person with such an unusual name. He died in an auto accident, but I don't know anything other than that." She said, "Ollie wants you to telephone his mother and tell her you talked to him." I said, "No way, unless he gives me some evidence it is really him." I then asked, "What kind of car was he driving when he had the accident?" Through her he said, "I was not driving. A friend was driving me home from a wrestling match when I fell asleep against the door handle and fell out at 60 miles per hour. The car was an old Duesenberg."

With that information, I telephoned his mother, who I had known for many years. I thought she would freak out, but to my surprise, she said she has seen her son and felt his presence around her house many times. I was glad that was not traumatic for her, so I asked what kind of car he was in when he died. She said she didn't know, but she would telephone the family of the boy who was driving. A week later, she called to say they were in an old Duesenberg that night! Finally, evidence of real spirit communication, for no one in our group knew that information, including me.

After I was convinced of the validity of communicating with spirits, I lost interest in the class because I didn't have any loved ones in the spirit world, and I felt most people in our group took the whole thing too seriously. My observation at the time was that all the malcontents I had known on the material plane ended up in the spirit world, and they were still malcontents!

Reverend Panton reinforced that observation by explaining that going into the spirit world doesn't make someone smarter or wiser, or more spiritually evolved. In fact, he said, "Spiritual progress in the spirit world is not possible because challenges and obstructions do not exist there." As in a dream, whatever you can conceive in the spirit world is instantly manifested, so how can there be soul growth in that unobstructed realm? We all return to this material plane where challenges, and especially pain, stimulate further evolution and eventual transcendence.

I also observed that the spirit world and the dream world are both, for the most part, self-created states. There is not one spirit world and not one dream world where we all go every night. Each person creates his own spirit world to some extent. When two people are sleeping in the same bed, and both are in the dream world, it doesn't mean they are sharing anything.

On the other hand, dream researchers have conducted laboratory sleep experiments where mentalists sent a specific mental image to people who were sleeping, and upon waking them, the ones sleeping reported dreaming about what the mentalist had projected. Some communication is possible, but overall, it appeared to me that a person's dream experiences, like the experiences in the spirit world, are a personal creation and not necessarily connected to anyone, as was revealed to me in one of our classes.

One night, my great-grandmother came to me through someone, and I asked how my grandfather was doing. She said she was just talking to him and he was fine. Two minutes later, my grandfather came to me through another person in the class. I asked him how his mother was doing, and he said he hadn't seen her in quite a while. The movie, *What Dreams May Come,* with Robin Williams, comes close to depicting the spirit world as I understand it to be.

The Tibetan Book of the Dead gives the best description of the various transitions one encounters after dying, but it is couched in a psychic and religious context that is not easy for most Westerners to understand.

When the time comes, here is a modern-day practice I learned that could possibly ease the transition into the spirit world for some people. The way to do this practice is to stay conscious during the transitions between the three states: waking, dreaming, and deep-sleeping. Almost everyone goes unconscious when changing frequencies to the dream state, and they have no idea how they got there. Even lucid dreamers, or people who claim they can consciously manipulate their dreams, are already within their dream before attempting to co-create it.

Most beginning lucid dreamers take great delight in controlling their dreams because they have not learned the importance of not interfering with their dreams. While we sleep, one of the many processes of our higher selves is to try to organize and make meaning of our lives.

If you can stay aware through that transition, it will aid you when the time comes to die because the transitions to the dream state and the spirit world are similar. Both are simply a change of frequency, and both are a higher frequency than the waking state. The dream and spirit world are similar realms where thoughts are things and time is fluid.

There are no steps in this practice other than trying to stay aware through the transitions. Begin by feeling what it is like to be awake. Then feel the subtle change in vibration as you transition to the dream state, and stay aware of it as it continues. All frequencies are available simultaneously, so it is just a matter of tuning into the dream state frequency to open up the dream world. When you get good at consciously tuning in instead of letting it happen unconsciously, there will be no confusion when entering the spirit world. There will be no wandering around in an interim frequency scaring people who are only tuned to the material plane frequencies.

The next big transition is between the dream state and the deep-sleep state. When you become familiar with how that feels, the transition from the spirit world frequencies to the Great Oneness or void is easy. That frequency is so high, it feels like stillness and is often expressed as nothingness. Then, of course, coming out of deep sleep and going into another dream or to the waking state is similar to being reborn out of the Great Oneness to another incarnation in a physical body. Be the nothingness until you feel the "awake" state taking over again.

Here is how I sometimes experience coming out of deep sleep and tuning from nothingness into the waking state frequency. First come a kaleidoscope of colors – vague, translucent, wispy, pastel colors slowly flowing then solidifying into the sharp, distinct, layered colors of the rainbow. Sounds are also muffled, distant, and diffuse until they jell into more distinct and recognizable forms: "Ah, birds are singing outside my window."

All sensations are more harsh and distinct in the waking state/material realm than in the other two more subtle realms.

Being born from the dark, fluid, insulated world of the womb into the harsh world of gravity and extreme sensations outside the womb can be shocking at first. It is no wonder that most of us come into this world crying. I distinctly remember the harshness of the hospital lights even though my eyelids were closed, and the painfully loud sounds of metal instruments being put away hurt my ears. Also, the coldness of the air and the hardness of that damn metal weighing scale they put me on were also painful.

There is no need to fear dying or being born. The more conscious the transitional processes become, the easier the transitions. And remember, the lower frequencies are no less divine than the others. They are just another Playground for the Playful. I also want to emphasize that no matter how high a frequency you can embrace, there will always be ones higher still to experience and integrate.

Your inherent divine nature is capable of being aware of all frequencies and all transitions.

Why limit yourself to so few?

This practice will confirm that the waking, dreaming, and deep-sleep states are similar to the material world, the spiritual world, and the void. What you experience in a 24-hour period is parallel to what you will experience when you transition between life in a physical body, to life in the spirit world, to life in the void, and back to the material world.

We eventually discontinued the class, and Malcolm never did any more psychic training. It was strictly Vedanta from that time on, and that was fine with me. Malcolm never did psychic stuff for its own sake. He used it to show us there is more to life than what we encounter in the physical world, and his class certainly did that for me.

Learning to Play with Earnly

Earnly Magnussen Panton was the power behind the Vedanta Center and a force of nature. When she entered a room, those present would intuitively look up to see who had changed the energetic field of that space. She never said much, but when she did, people paid attention.

She spoke with the authority that came from years of commanding respect from everyone who knew her.

The circumstances and details of her life are so unusual, even Malcolm said he was never sure he got the sequence right. We called a meeting and recorded all those who had known her. The following is a composite of everyone's recollections – including hers:

Earnly was born in 1901 in a burning building in Bergen, Norway. She and her mother were rescued just before the house burned to the ground. That auspicious beginning was indicative of her entire life.

She lived with a burning perfectionism and the skills to manifest it. That drive and talent propelled her to the heights of whatever interested her – only to have that endeavor dashed to pieces. Then another career would be launched into the stratosphere with the same results. By the time I met her, she had been living a life of moderation for nearly 20 years and was at peace with herself. She certainly got there the hard way. The following is my best attempt to order her "many lifetimes" within her present life.

One of Earnly's biggest challenges was the fact she was born with so many extraordinary talents – a prodigy in dance, mathematics, chess, singing, and by the time I met her, she was a highly respected artist. She also had many paranormal abilities, the most unusual of which was that she seemed to live an entire lifetime every decade.

She became an accomplished ballet dancer for both the Royal Danish Ballet and the Imperial Ballet in St. Petersburg, Russia before the age of ten! That was where the Russian ballerina Anna Pavlova danced the Dying Swan in 1905. Earnly said she idolized Anna.

Her family moved to the US, where she landed a two-picture contract with Fox Studios. In those days, the studio had a live fox as a mascot and due to Earnly's lifelong infatuation with animals, she got too close to the fox, and he bit her on the mouth and nearly tore off her upper lip. That abruptly ended her acting career. Her scar was still noticeable when I knew her.

She studied flamenco dancing, and Indian classical dance with the famous Uday Shankar. And, she spent a good deal of time dancing in the Ziegfeld Follies.

Amidst all that dancing, when she was 17, she met and secretly married a famous Italian opera singer. Most of her students thought he might have been Enrico Caruso, but she never mentioned his name because she said she jumped out of the taxi on their return from the wedding ceremony and never saw him again until their annulment seven years later. She never did say why she ran away from him on their wedding day.

She began interpretive dancing in her mid-twenties. George Gershwin invited her to dance at his pre-opening of *Rhapsody in Blue* in Aeolian Hall. Gershwin's friends liked her dance routine more than his new orchestrated piece, and he fired her after that one performance.

Her dancing career ended tragically when she tore herself in half while jumping up to kick the back of her head. At the time, she was one of only a few people in the world who could do it. She nearly died and lay unmoving in the hospital for six months. She said she lost so much weight the doctors brought their anatomy classes to her bedside to use her as a reference!

She recovered in Bucks County, Pennsylvania, gardening with her mother. Thomas Edison's niece moved in next door, and she became good friends with their family.

They, in turn, introduced her to Edison and his wife Mina. I know that because one day, we all went to the Edison museum in Ft. Myers, Florida where she suddenly exclaimed, "That is the electric car Mina and I used to ride around in!"

Concurrently with her dancing career, she made a name for herself as a mathematical prodigy and board game strategist. She was often invited to solve math problems at the private colleges she attended and often solved them without calculation. She would write the final equation without any interim steps. She said it sometimes took them weeks to fill in the middle of her equations.

Also, in her mid-twenties, while traveling on one of her family's Norwegian cruise ships from South America to Cuba to New York, she repeatedly beat a famous chess master who asked that she not tell anyone because he claimed to have not been beaten in tournament chess for years. He said that her not giving any thought to her moves unnerved him. (I suspect the chess master was José Capablanca.)

Another paranormal ability allowed her to run in a trance state nonstop from 42nd Street to the Battery Tunnel in Manhattan every night after work. Once she set a target to run to, she could not stop. She claimed that her feet only lightly touched the pavement. She later read of Tibetan runners doing the same thing while running several hundred miles at a time.

In her late twenties, while visiting relatives in Cuba and attending the University of Havana, she joined students in a political rally. From atop an overturned burning bus, she gave an impassioned speech and became co-leader of an entire mini-revolution. She barely escaped with her life. Her father rescued her because he had become a secret agent for our government and knew exactly what was happening.

I have been to Cuba many times, and each time I try to research that revolution. The historians I consulted all said the same thing, "There was a revolution every few months at that time in Cuba's history, so we have no idea which one it was."

She started her short singing career after the Cuban experience, which lasted throughout her early thirties. She discovered she had a coloratura voice and had bookings all over the world. However (there is always a "however" in her life), a jealous singer gave her a drink laced with strychnine, which burned her throat.

When I knew her, every time she got stressed, she would lose her voice and always blamed it on the strychnine. She is lucky that it was only her inability to speak occasionally that she lost.

Earnly at 30

Meanwhile, while visiting relatives in Chicago, she and her mother had a few dinners with Al Capone, but neither of them liked him. However, Earnly did say she dated John Dillinger several times because he was always a gentleman with her.

She claimed she was indirectly involved in his famous shoot-out at the theater. John and his new girlfriend were to meet her across the street in her apartment, but detectives broke in and pushed her down and started to shoot at poor John out her window. (If you think this is hard to believe, wait until you read what my Daoist master was capable of doing.)

After all that excitement, she eventually married a Mexican lawyer and lived quietly on a farm in Connecticut. Soon after, he died of a heart attack while talking to her on the phone. It was then she decided to enter a Buddhist nunnery and retreat from the world. After taking a vow of renunciation, she learned from her relatives that she had inherited the family fortune! Apparently, her father had money stashed away in banks all over Norway. She dropped the renunciation clause and tried to claim the money but learned the Nazis had taken it to Germany.

It was around that time she met Malcolm at a psychic fair, and both their lives changed drastically. With his prompting, she began a painting career, which continued through her late forties and early fifties. This included their move from New York to St. Petersburg, Florida. She had many large showings in New York and in Florida, but she had stopped painting by the time I showed up.

My fondest memories of her were when she came out to their center at night to coach me when I was learning to play the piano. Her coaching was an intimate experience for me because she guided me from within. Sometimes I felt like a puppet being moved. She would say things like, "You can think about that later" or, "If you change your attitude, that piece will sound completely different." Her soft voice coming out of the darkness affected me strongly. Until then, I had not known humans were capable of that particular level of intimacy. I spent nearly a decade with Earnly and Malcolm, off and on from 1963 to 1973. A few years after I left their center to study Daoism in California, Malcolm had a freak accident. He was in their kitchen making breakfast when his silk bathrobe caught fire over the gas stove. He was badly burned and died shortly thereafter. What a shock to us all. Even after that horrific experience, Earnly continued teaching her Yoga classes until she died peacefully at age 82.

The circumstances surrounding her death on February 26, 1983, were as spectacular as her birth and life. It is common knowledge in spiritual circles that when a person of high spiritual evolution dies, there is often an unusual wind that surrounds the house or area in which they lived. Nature's response to Earnly's death is the most documented and unusual "wind" story I have ever heard.

In her case, the headlines of the St. Petersburg newspaper devoted the entire top half of the front page describing the unusual hurricane winds that rocked the city the day after she died.

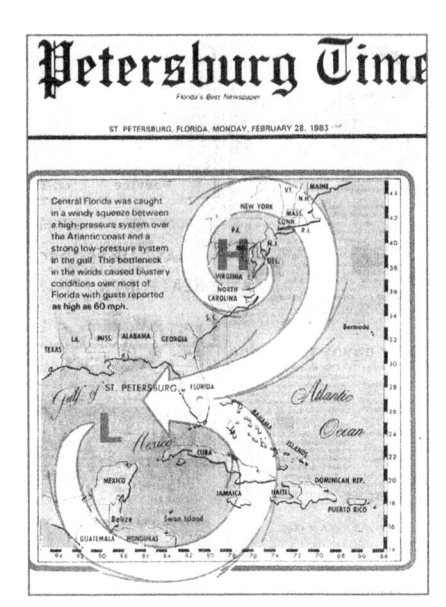

The article described the unseasonable winds originating in the New York area, swirling clockwise to the south and hitting St. Pete from the East. That wind was met by winds coming up from the vicinity of Cuba, swirling counterclockwise, and joining the winds from New York.

Here is the clincher: That newspaper drawing closely matched the Hindu symbol for Om, which was on the sign outside of their center. Everyone at the center knew that was no coincidence. She had always considered New York and Cuba as her other homes.

So what, you say? Why go into so much detail? Many talented people who are not spiritually evolved lead extraordinary lives, and conversely, a great soul like Ramana Maharshi did nothing unusual in the course of his life and yet an entire city grew up around him in southern India. I simply want you to know that such persons exist and to encourage you to find someone who inspires you as they inspired me.

What did I learn about Play from the Pantons? On the way to them, I learned about the magic of synchronicity. From them, I learned:

The power of love, presence, and fearlessness – three more important ingredients in a life of Play.

From the Pantons, and from all of my other teachers, I learned that love is not the sentimental drivel that most people think it is. In its highest expression, love involves complete identity with everything. It is similar to what happens when my left hand is cut and the right hand bandages it. Does the right hand feel good about having done so? Is it expressing love to the other hand? Or is it simply a natural response that comes from a sense of identity with the other? Earnly and Malcolm used to say, "If you are able to go through life as God's right hand and experience everything else as being God's left hand, then you will be compassionate with all creatures."

Also, the power of presence is something to behold when you meet someone who has it. This power manifests when someone's whole being is entirely present in every moment. When that vastness focuses, the resulting intensity is awesome. Speaking of awesome, the Pantons also used to say, "If a person loses their sense of awe, awful things will happen to them."

To be in the presence of someone with that intensity is to feel that nothing exists except that moment because, from the standpoint of the person focusing that vastness, nothing else does exist. I have never met anyone I considered capable of Play that didn't have that intensity of focus.

Fearlessness is also another facet of Play that expressed itself repeatedly in the Pantons' lives. Their motto was, "Fling yourself into life and live wholeheartedly. You only have 50 million lifetimes, so make the most of it." Not only did their early lives reflect a fearlessness to venture into the unknown, after they met, they continued that trend by building a bridge between East and West long before anyone else was doing it.

The downside to being fearless and multi-talented is the tendency to overlook the need for caution and moderation. Earnly certainly had a talent for pushing the envelope in everything she did. The need for moderation is one of the fundamental principles of life in the Orient, and it is clear to me that it is one of the most needed lessons we in the West need to learn.

I later learned the energetic principle behind moderation. Many years later, my Daoist teacher told me that whenever you push yin or yang to its limit, it will reverse itself. This is an invariant law of nature. My psychiatrist friends gave credence to that theory by pointing out that manic-depressives are perfect examples of living life to the extreme. They are unbelievably creative and agitated one minute, then horribly listless and depressed the next. The energy that goes into creating the extreme high causes a corresponding low. That is when things inevitably reverse themselves. They then find themselves in a pit and wonder how they got there. It is not a mystery. That kind of life can wear you out in a hurry. The only way to avoid the pits is to not shoot into the stratosphere when you are feeling good. As the Daoists have long said, "Round out the extremes in your life, and it will be long and sweet."

How often have you seen overly aggressive, outgoing people end their lives in seclusion and fear? Adolf Hitler and Howard Hughes come to mind. Hitler's Third Reich was supposed to last a thousand years but ended just twelve years later with Hitler hunkered in a bunker. Macho Hughes had every woman he ever wanted. He also had all the money and influence a man could hope for. But by the time he died, he looked like a little old lady with his shawl around his shoulders – living in isolation. He suffered from obsessive-compulsive disorder and paranoia. He was also afraid of every disease known at the time. He was down to 93 pounds, took 20 aspirins a day, and only drank milk. He is a perfect example of exaggerated yang changing into yin.

Conversely, how many times have people who espoused "turning the other cheek" and other forms of extreme pacifism died violently? (Jesus, Gandhi, Martin Luther King Jr., etc.) How many overly zealous missionaries preached only love and peace – yet only horror followed in their wake? Most of us do not have the karma Earnly had nor the opportunity of living an entire lifetime every decade, so the principle of moderation is not as apparent in our lives as it was in hers. Most of us need many incarnations to realize the profundity and necessity of leading a life of moderation. Use her early life as an example that even an incredibly gifted person cannot sustain living in the extreme for any length of time before it reverses itself. If I had not eventually learned the details of her early life, I would have never suspected that the contented, unhurried, unassuming "little old lady" that was such a stabilizing influence in my life had lived such an extreme life when she was young. Her life is living proof that:

Living a life of moderation is a major factor in a life of Play.

LEARNING TO PLAY WITH OTHER TEACHERS

Malcolm and Earnly were not the only strong influences in my life at that time. Various spiritual teachers visiting our Vedanta center influenced me as well. Pir Vilayat Inayat Khan dropped by several times and taught Universal Sufism, which views all religions as rays of light from the same sun. Philip Kapleau stopped by once. He was a Zen Buddhist teacher who taught the Sanbo Kyodan tradition, blending all the schools of Zen. The great Hatha Yoga practitioner Vishnudevananda frequented our center. He founded the Sivananda Yoga Vedanta Centre in both Montreal and Nassau. I visited his place in Nassau.

I also traveled to France to visit Vedanta centers. In a small ashram outside Paris, I met the most loving individual I have ever known. His name was Ritajananda. When he heard I was a student of the Pantons, he insisted I sit next to him on his bed while he recovered from an illness. He lay there silently, holding my hands in his hands as tears of love and rapture streamed down his face. That went on for several days.

All those people influenced me to some degree, and each possessed certain aspects of Play, but I didn't feel that any of them had the total package I was looking for. I had to wait until I met my Chinese teacher to find that. I suppose I didn't meet him sooner because I simply wasn't ready.

I was preoccupied with cultivating an integrated, balanced healthy ego because no one can transcend a sick ego. I first had to become somebody before I became nobody under my Zen teacher and eventually became everybody under my Daoist teacher.

Another strong influence on me in those days, which had nothing to do with Vedanta, was my first long-term relationship with a woman. I met her at a graphics party, and it was love at first touch. You can learn only so much about yourself from being one with the Universe, but if you want to know more, then live with a woman.

I had everything in the entire cosmos figured out in those days except for women. They seemed like such overly emotional, irrational creatures, and yet they knew things I didn't have a clue about. They were constantly exposing my lack of tact, non-existent social skills, and my state of arrested adolescence. They also kept accusing me of acting like I was the center of the Universe. Little did those silly creatures know that any fool could think they are the center of the Universe, but it takes a real sage to know they are the entirety of the Universe. If truth be told (and it seldom is), I honestly didn't know I was such a pain in the ass until I got involved with that wild, Italian woman and her pesky daughter, who I nicknamed "Screech" for obvious reasons. I am a sucker for Italian women, Sophia Loren being my ideal. Throughout my short and not very distinguished career, I have been desperately searching for that certain spiritual quality that only Italian women seem to possess. You would think I would mature beyond that little obsession – but no. Our relationship was great for several years, and I learned more about myself from her than I did with all my previous teachers. But one day, she surprised me by not being willing to uproot her life and follow me to California when I got the urge to travel.

In spite of my love for Vedanta, the Pantons, and my wonderful relationship, I was ripe for something new. A strong discontent stirred within me. My restlessness was traceable to how comfortable and predictable my life had become. The adage, "familiarity breeds contempt," seemed to fit my situation at the time. Nowadays, I simply say, "familiarity breeds!"

After reading a few books on Daoism, I noticed my attention was turning more and more to the Chinese in general, and to the Daoists in particular. I was impressed with how natural and practical their religion was and how it kept their lives in perspective and in balance.

Near the end of my eighth year at the Vedanta Center, I announced I had learned as much as I could while there, and told them I was drifting toward Daoism. I heard that the only Daoist centers in the United States were out West, so I bid a loving and respectful adieu to everyone and headed westward to find some Daoists. Little did I know I would be returning to their center within a year.

Learning to Play at the Tassajara Zen Center

A funny thing happened on my way to finding Daoists. I never found any. I ended up a practicing Buddhist instead.

After securing a cheap apartment in Los Angeles, I worked odd jobs because I couldn't find anything in graphics (and besides, being odd made me perfectly suitable for that work). On the weekends, I drove around California looking for Daoists. However, as synchronicity would have it, I stumbled upon a Zen Center in Tassajara that was run by Shunryu Suzuki Roshi, one of the most prominent men to bring Zen Buddhism to the United States. I was so fascinated by the man, I returned every weekend for about a year. His personality did not attract me as much as what he evoked within me. Things did not go well at first, but eventually, it was smooth sailing right into the Buddhist Void.

His center was in the middle of nowhere and difficult to find. The road was washed out the day I arrived, so I had to abandon my camper and walk in. Upon arrival, I announced that if the spirit of Zen was as hard to find as this place, I was in for a difficult time. My first day there seemed to substantiate that feeling.

After passing a verbal quiz that allowed me to sit with the professional meditators, I settled into one of their rustic cabins in a gorgeous river canyon somewhere southeast of Carmel-by-the-Sea. Although I had never before been in a river canyon, the first thing I decided to do was to hit the trail. I climbed the steep canyon wall and got stranded halfway up. People swimming in the river heard my cries for help and managed to get me down after a lot of teasing. It was an embarrassing but perhaps auspicious beginning. Was I spiritually climbing too steeply and rapidly with only my Vedanta background as support? Nah!

My next challenge was an assignment to work in the kitchen. I was accustomed to feeding myself at fast-food stores while traveling and eating TV dinners at home. The cooks in the kitchen got their first clue I was no gourmet chef when they saw me salivating every time one of them crinkled tinfoil around me (the Pavlovian response of a TV dinner addict). Since I was useless in the kitchen, they agreed to let me sweep the grounds – under close supervision, of course.

I may not have been competent in those rustic settings, but once I got on my little black cushion, I felt like I was in my natural environment once again. Just sit quietly and stare at the wall – not a bad way to spend a day.

Because the Roshi was mostly trained in the Soto Zen sect, we all meditated facing the wall. (Practitioners in the Rinzai School sit facing each other.) A student with a long, flat paddle would patrol the aisle between us and whack us on the shoulders when we dozed off or when we signaled we wanted a little stimulation. I repeated that routine most weekends for several months, interspersed with talks by the Roshi, which I later discovered were put into a book called *Zen Mind, Beginner's Mind*.

The first time I saw him, I was surprised how small and frail he was. When I learned he was battling cancer, I savored every moment with him. Although his countenance was unassuming and approachable, we never spoke to each other except to say "hi." Zen practitioners can be quite stiff and formal, but I always felt relaxed and comfortable around him. After a few occasions of sitting with him and his group, I experienced the Buddhist Void, or at least that is what I thought it was. Every time I was in his presence for a few hours, a deep stillness came over me, and occasionally I felt myself dissolve into a brilliant blackness.

I don't know any other way to describe it. It was not exactly black, nor was it nothingness. Actually, it was one of the more intense and powerful non-experiences I ever had. I call them non-experiences because if the person having the experience dissolves in the process, whatever happens cannot, strictly speaking, be considered an experience. Only after I remanifested could I refer to the non-experience. From this, I intuited the Void was full of energy and creativity, certainly not the nothingness most people describe.

Have you ever played with an oscilloscope? It is a machine showing time intervals between electrical pulses as a curved line wiggles above and below the median line. You can crank up the frequency to where the peaks and troughs seem to stand still due to the incredible speed of the vibration. In other words, the movement becomes so fast, it appears as if it is not moving. The still Void felt a bit like that.

Meanwhile, back at the Zen Center, I arrived for a weekend in December when I got the news the Roshi had died. Toward

Suzuki Roshi

the latter part of the year, he had stayed in San Francisco because of failing health, so his death was not surprising to anyone. However, that didn't lessen the loss I felt, even though I continued to feel his presence.

I mostly miss his stories. He would sip tea as he talked, and sometimes the sip lasted several minutes between sentences. To be that unhurried and content, even though he was dying, was quite remarkable. After he died, I felt alone and isolated, so I returned to Florida and the Vedanta center. I stayed there another two years, even though I was still restless for change.

Playing with Daoists in Colorado

It was mid-1973, when Alan Watts, the British philosopher and writer on Eastern religions, called to announce I was a co-winner in his essay contest. For decades, I had been impressed with his concise, lucid writing style. When he invited his fans to write about why we wanted to study with him, I could not resist. The prize was to work in his library on his houseboat in Sausalito, California. I headed out west again just as fast as I could to claim my prize.

Along the way, I briefly stopped in Manitou Springs, Colorado, to visit the Still Point Daoist Center run by Gia-Fu Feng and Jane English. I liked their book on the Dao Duh Jing (my phonetic spelling of the Tao Te Ching – the bible of the Daoists). Although I had already read many versions of the Dao Duh Jing, I thought theirs was especially well-photographed, more concise than most, and since I had just completed a few semesters studying Chinese in

Florida, I appreciated his calligraphy on each page.

When they heard where I was going, they told me they were married by Alan Watts and claimed their ceremony began with him saying, "Do you realize your love for each other will grow less and less as the years go by?" I appreciate a good sense of humor.

Much to our horror, Alan died during my visit to their center. Was his death a message from the Universe? If so, what should I do? After giving it much thought, I decided to do nothing.

Gia-Fu Feng

I would have stayed at the Still Point Center longer than I did, but I soon realized it should have been named the Center of the Hurricane! Both Gia-Fu and Jane were a bit eccentric for my taste, and the whole place seemed a little nuts. He spent much of his time floating in an old bathtub on the mountain trail and she was focused on her photography.

There was not a shred of Daoism being practiced there. At night, they practiced Fritz Perls' brand of psychotherapy. Since that school of psychology puts an emphasis on "getting in touch with your true inner feelings," those sentiments frequently played out during the day.

It was common to find that someone had expressed "their true inner feelings" by throwing all our shoes off the porch into the valley below. It once took me two days to find my other sneaker.

Each night we went to a large room with a chair in the middle with pillows circling the "hot seat." Whoever sat in that chair was prodded to reveal all their life secrets. Rage and sadness ensued with much crying and pillow shredding. Except for me, of course.

One night I agreed to sit in the hot seat, and after everyone took a turn assessing me (without much accuracy), I went around the room in what seemed like a semi-trance state. I only said a few words to everyone about what I sensed about them, but it was enough to set off half the people in the room into a rage, and the other half started crying. I have no idea what I said.

A few days after hearing my "true inner feelings" about them, they asked me to leave. I left a few days later when I heard about the only other Daoist center in the United States at that time. It was called the Taoist Sanctuary and was run by the famous *E Jing (I Ching)* scholar, Khigh Dhiegh, in Los Angeles.

Playing at the Taoist Sanctuary in Los Angeles

The sanctuary was a rented Christian church in North Hollywood, built in the shape of a big "U." We used to practice our Tai Ji and Kung Fu in the central courtyard. The small rooms that made up the "U" shape were for all the various classes.

Chinese ceremonies, weddings, *E Jing*, and philosophical Daoist studies were going on constantly. Each faction had a designated time. We would meet as a group only for holidays, celebrations, and to demonstrate our skills to the public. We mixed more like a tossed salad than a melting pot, and it was all held together by Khigh Dhiegh, the *E Jing* expert.

You might recognize him as the actor who played the villain Wo Fat in the original *Hawaii Five-O* TV series. People who came to his sanctuary said they could not imagine such wisdom coming out of the mouth of the evil "Wo Fat."

He often replied, "Acting as an *E Jing* scholar is one of my more challenging roles. Wo Fat is much closer to my real self." I agreed with his self-assessment and did not feel he was as highly evolved as Earnly or Suzuki Roshi, but he certainly knew the *E Jing*.

Khigh was not the only instructor at the sanctuary. June Yuer taught Tai Ji, Chao Li Chi taught classes in Daoism, and Master Share K. Lew taught Gung Fu classes.

Khigh Dhiegh

What a cast of characters those three were!

June was a tough, smallish blond artist by nature with hair the length of her back. She could bend over with her legs straight and touch her nose to her toes! I am not exaggerating. Having a big nose, short legs, and a long waist helped, but she certainly could do it.

Because June often reminded me of Earnly, she became my favorite teacher.

I never had much interaction with Share K. Lew because I had no interest in Gung Fu. There was always a slight tension between the classy Tai Ji students and the

June Yuer

Gung Fu thugs. One day when we were demonstrating for the public, a Gung Fu practitioner dropped his sword and miraculously caught it before it hit the ground. He said, "See what incredible reflexes we develop by practicing Gung Fu." I shouted from the audience, "A Tai Ji practitioner would never have dropped it in the first place!" And so it went. Because we all called ourselves Daoists, we managed to keep from strangling each other.

I started studying many versions of the Dao Duh Jing, and Tai Ji replaced Yoga in my life. I also started a relationship with a woman I met in a calligraphy class. For the first few classes, she and I spent most of our time making ink together. Don't snicker – grinding an ink stick down to a liquid can be quite sensual. My main interest at the sanctuary was the study of the *E Jing* (once again, my phonetic spelling of the I Ching). I immersed myself in that book for over two years, and I still regard it as the most profound book I have ever studied.

The fact that China managed to produce a book that both the Daoists and Confucianists hold in high regard is proof of its profundity. Those two camps have been antagonists for centuries. The Confucianists are stuffy legalist, ritual performing, social-order fanatics. The Daoists are more profound, spontaneous, and easy-going. (Or, so I say from the perspective of a "fair and balanced" Daoist.) Confucius himself said that if he had another 50 years to live, he would have devoted it entirely to the study of the *E Jing*. I agree with him because I have studied and taught it for the past 30 years and have only scratched the surface.

Chao Li Chi

Chao Li Chi was an actor and a Chinese scholar from whom I studied Daoism and learned the ancient meanings and evolution of many Chinese characters. He performed my wedding ceremony 15 years later.

The *E Jing* has its origins in antiquity. Fu Shi, a mythological character, is credited with originating the solid and broken lines that represent the 64 variations of the energies of Yin and Yang. Each energetic situation is a hexagram with six layers.

Much later, King Wen and the Duke of Chou (Jou) are credited with putting the meanings into the various hexagrams. A thousand years later, Confucius discovered the hexagrams. He and his disciples added more commentaries, which caught on like wildfire, and rightly so. The *E Jing* can inspire and counsel a person like nothing else. It is like having a wise friend with you at all times. It reveals how change occurs in the Universe by utilizing the power of similar energies to resonate with each other. For example, if you ask a question in the context of fear, the *E Jing* will respond to the powerful fear frequency instead of the question. So be open and willing to accept any response you get, and if you are open, the response can be astoundingly relevant to your question. Each of the 64 hexagrams is composed of six unique combinations of those two complementary forces of nature, Yin and Yang. An enormous amount of information can be learned from each hexagram if you know how to interpret different energetic combinations. The hexagrams not only respond to your question, they can show you what a particular situation will evolve into. Every morning at the same time, we were given an assignment to ask the *E Jing*, "What is my energy composition today?" We were encouraged to do this for two years. When we all gathered together to read the results, we were astounded to see that each of us had a clear record of our energy cycles during that time, and each person had a unique cycle of repetition. Some of the students discovered they had injuries on the same day every year. Others had a very consistent ebb and flow of energy throughout the year, while others had abrupt changes punctuated with extreme fluctuations. It was fascinating to see our individual cycles. When people asked Khigh why the Daoists stopped at 64 situations instead of going into the next phase of 128, he said, "The Divine created all biological life with only 64 nucleic acids. So, if 64 was good enough for God, it is good enough for me." Although the *E Jing* is regarded as an oracle by most of its adherents, Khigh often said that the idea is to eventually throw the book away and become a living *E Jing*. In other words, develop your own intuition until you know with confidence how to respond appropriately to every circumstance. It was all quite stimulating at the sanctuary, and the atmosphere there was quite far off the Vedanta and Zen centers.

It was about that time I started to appreciate the many subtle differences between those three great religions. Most of the differences were only a matter of how to attain and manifest the great Oneness. I was much more comfortable with the Daoist approach, and these are the differences as I experienced them: Daoism is the only religion indigenous to China. I do not consider Confucianism a religion because it has no transcendent aspect. It is mostly a system of how to live your life morally and ethically. Vedanta and Buddhism originated in India. With a few exceptions, their practitioners are "strivers" to the core. The Vedantists strive to transcend the world of "things" and want to get off the cycle of rebirths (reincarnation) to return to the great Oneness. The Buddhists strive to get beyond pain by transcending the ego. The crazy Daoists, on the other hand, flow rather than strive and want to live on Earth as long as possible. They maintain that if you live right – integrally, authentically, moderately, and selflessly – you won't have much pain. If you "realize" (to make real) the world of manifestation is an expression of the great Oneness, then there is no conflict between the two and no need to go or to stay anywhere. The tension between the great Oneness and the manifest world just dissolves. It is not solved, as in solving a problem; it simply dissolves because there was no problem in the first place. There is another important reason why the Daoists want to live a long time, and it is mostly a practical matter. They point out that in an average incarnation, a person gets less than 10 years out of 72 to make any kind of spiritual progress. The first 18 years are usually lived unconsciously, which was certainly the case with me. The second 18 years are spent securing a career and a family. The third 18 years are exhausted raising the kids. The last 18 years are the only ones available for spiritual progress, but usually health concerns dominate until you die. If you could add another 72 years of radiant health to your newly acquired wisdom by living to 144, you could spare yourself the grind of reincarnating every 72 years. The Daoists call it "the old meat-and-bones rotation."

Another significant difference between Daoism and other Religions is its acceptance of chaos and mystery (all things dark and mysterious). Daoists seem to want to know and experience everything, and that includes the unknown and the chaotic. Most religions and civilizations battle with and repress chaos, while the Daoists embrace it. Hun Dun (Chaos) is accepted as an important aspect of the innate creativity and spontaneity of life, so of course, the Daoists want to know it and live it. Their interest in the silent, dark aspects of life reminds me of the famous dog story in *The Memoirs of Sherlock Holmes*.

In it, Holmes draws the attention of the Scotland Yard detective to "the curious incident of the dog in the night," to which the detective remarks, "The dog did nothing in the nighttime." Holmes replies, "That was the curious incident." The dog not barking meant the dog knew the killer, which was a significant clue to solving the case.

In a similar way, listening to the silent, mysterious, chaotic, dark forces of Nature yields clues to the fundamental principles of the Universe. I recently heard that so-called Dark matter and Dark energy comprise 96 percent of the mass of the Universe, yet they are called "Dark" because physicists know so little about these forces. How can we hope to learn more about the Universe if we do not understand 96 percent of it? How can anyone truly Play if they are not familiar with the dark, chaotic forces that so strongly influence our lives?

It was also at that time I became obsessed with understanding one of the more mysterious aspects of the Universe – holograms. No matter how hard I tried, I could not understand how a small piece of an image could contain the entirety of the image and, at the same time, lend itself to the total picture. So I took a course at UCLA in making holograms. What we made were not the cheap, laminated holograms available today. We did it the old-fashioned way. We used silver-covered glass plates like the first photographers used, and, if the lasers moved as little as three-millionths of an inch in the process, we lost the entire image. I made a three-dimensional image in space of a globe of the Earth. If you look at the glass without a laser light going through it, you see what appears to be a wood grain pattern, which is the chaotic interference pattern out of which the image emerges. If you look at the top of the glass plate with monochromatic laser light going through it, you can see the globe with the North Pole showing. If you look at the bottom of the plate, you can see the South Pole. So I cut off a piece of the glass plate near the bottom and looked through it, and there was the entire globe in that small piece of glass as seen from the perspective of the South Pole. Wow! From a chaotic pattern, you can construct a three-dimensional globe complete with continents. I still can't understand how that is technically possible, but even today, as I stare at it, I get it intuitively. With science exploring the mysterious world of quantum physics, the dark and mysterious realms of the Universe are giving up their secrets. Before long, everyone will be as excited about the dark forces of Nature as the Daoists have long been, and quantum physicists are now. What I learned from the holographic effect is that we are part of the Universe AND the totality of it. Don't go around thinking you are merely a drop of water in the vast Ocean.

You are the vast Ocean manifesting through a drop of water!

Just as I looked through the small piece of the hologram and saw the entire globe, you too contain the entire Universe within yourself.

In spite of all that new and interesting stuff at the Taoist Sanctuary, I was not overly impressed with anyone I knew there as compared to the caliber of the people I had already known. I started looking around to see what else the West Coast offered in the way of enlightened beings.

I sat with Muktananda, a Hindu guru, a few times, and he touched me with his peacock feathers (Shaktipat), but I simply didn't like the guy. Later I heard he got embroiled in sexual scandals. I visited the famous Hindu philosopher Krishnamurti in Ojai, California, and listened to him talk several times, but I found him too impersonal. Ram Dass, a New Age celebrity, was everywhere, but I didn't feel he had anything to offer me. The more I looked around, the more I became convinced I was the only hope this planet had at that time. With an attitude like that, you know a humbling experience is not far off!

Messiah
of the Modern Age?

In late 1974, I again felt a growing urge to transcend and move on. Problem was, where was I to go since I was already one with the Universe? I was acutely aware that "wherever I went, there I was," but I couldn't say the same for my luggage. I kept losing it at the airports. Was the Universe giving me a message about my personal baggage, do you suppose? Nah!

The *E Jing* kept encouraging me to travel, and since I do not argue with the *E Jing*, I decided to start a spiritual center of my own in Australia. I had just finished reading a book that suggested we ourselves become a Christ while waiting for Jesus to return. At that moment, I decided to become the new Messiah for the Modern Age.

Since I was convinced the Northern hemisphere would be uninhabitable soon, I chose Australia to be my new Mecca. The apocalyptic feeling I had about the future of the Northern hemisphere shows how a person can project a pending inner upheaval onto the outside world.

I got travel films on Australia and, after much consideration, chose the city of Darwin as my new Playground. There, future devotees would bow down in the direction of my golden image nine times a day and circumambulate my huge mausoleum in case I died – which I seriously doubted I was capable of at that time. Since I wanted to spend one last holiday with my friends in Los Angeles, I scheduled a flight out in January of 1975.

What was left of Darwin after the typhoon struck.

With my airline ticket sitting on my TV, I sat down Christmas Eve to watch the news just as the announcer was describing what was left of Darwin! Apparently, Cyclone Tracy, an unseasonable storm, hit the city and destroyed it. Everyone was forced to evacuate.

I cashed in my ticket while mumbling to myself, "For God's sake, I get the idea. Even if my idea was a bit premature, you didn't have to destroy the whole damn city just to keep me from going there. A voice out of a burning bush would have sufficed." Then, I heard a voice say, "I don't use burning bushes anymore. I am more ecologically-minded these days."

Well, so much for all those millions of adoring devotees in Australia. Damn, I actually had the golden image of me already designed in my mind. It had to be a reclining figure because I get my

best spiritual inspirations when lying down watching cage fighting on TV.

This whole incident reminds me of my uncle saying, "I have seen a lot of wonderful things happen to me in this lifetime, but unfortunately, most of them never materialized."

The next week at the Daoist sanctuary, one of my fellow students, who was one of the first people in the West to study acupuncture, dropped in with an invitation to join him and his Chinese girlfriend to study acupuncture in China. A month later, we three were on a plane to southern Taiwan, where their teacher lived. It was on that trip I met my Daoist teacher, and once again, my life changed dramatically.

Meeting My Teacher / Dragon in Taiwan

After studying in Taiwan with my new friends for a few weeks, I decided they were too advanced for me.

I looked around for a teacher of my own. In a real estate office, of all places, I overheard talk about a local acupuncturist who spoke a little English and lived nearby, so I decided to investigate. I talked my friends into joining me even though they were satisfied with their teacher.

It was a stinking hot day in southern Taiwan in early 1975 when the three of us walked into the acupuncture clinic/ home of my future teacher. We rounded an ornate partition and saw a young-looking man sitting with his hands in his sleeves, resembling the leading male in a martial arts movie.

With his short crew cut and enlarged knuckles, he resembled many Gung Fu (phonetic for Kung Fu) fighters I had met. Yet his unwrinkled face, high forehead, and slender fingers suggested an intelligent, sensitive, and refined individual. He looked much younger than me – I was 33 then – so I figured I had nothing to learn from him. Later, I learned he was 47 at that time. I was glad I ignored my first impression and had decided to study with him.

As I looked around his clinic and home, I noticed many rare acupuncture books in his extensive library and many styles of calligraphy adorning the walls. His herbal room was also impressive, but I was most surprised by the scrolls of Han Shan, my favorite Chinese poet, hanging on every wall.

I figured anyone who liked Han Shan was okay by me. I later heard he felt that any Westerner who even knew of Han Shan was okay with him.

He, his wife, and two preteen boys lived on the second floor. Their living quarters were modest yet tastefully done, which I later found out was due to his Feng Shui training and his wife's innate good taste. The third floor was his shrine, where he conducted Sunday morning ceremonies for his dozen or so students. It was weeks before we were invited up there.

After exchanging pleasantries, we discovered he actually did speak a little English, and that expedited our getting to know him. I had so many questions I didn't know where to begin. As it turned out, I asked the most significant question I could have asked right off the bat.

I noticed he had a small bald spot on top of his head that looked deliberately placed, so I asked him why it was there. He nonchalantly explained that he was born talking and with total recall of his past lives. That upset his parents so much they took him to a Daoist shaman to rid him of his memories. The shaman burned incense on that spot, and it must have worked because he said he lost those memories until he was 13 when he met his former teachers again. In their presence, those memories came flooding back.

This story is not so hard to believe, considering he later demonstrated on numerous occasions he had a photographic memory and total recall of everything said or done to him. I soon realized that he was the first person in my life that qualified as being an Avatar (the great Oneness fully incarnated as a human being.)

Since the Hindu concept of an avatar is shared by most Daoists and is so misunderstood, I would like to explore it in a little more detail before continuing the story.

As far as I know, only two religions allow for the possibility of God incarnating fully as a human being: Hinduism and Christianity. Judaism and Islam are opposed to the idea, while the Buddhists and Daoists are indifferent or vague on the subject. In Tibetan Buddhism, one of the signs by which every Dalai Lama is chosen is his ability to recognize his personal possessions from a previous life. However, it has never been clear to me whether those potential Dalai Lamas were born knowing their divinity.

The Oneness incarnating as human is further complicated by the fact that avatars come in many guises, so they are often hard to recognize. If you are a Christian, there is no problem because there was only one God incarnate: Jesus – end of discussion. However, if you allow for the possibility that the Oneness has incarnated several times throughout history, as the Hindu scriptures acknowledge, then recognizing a saint or avatar can be problematic because you need some criteria to know who is and who isn't a true avatar.

Keep in mind the difference between saints and avatars. Saints are born in ignor(e)ance – ignoring their innate Godliness. Through effort and grace, they realize their own divinity. Avatars are incarnations of God, born knowing their divinity.

Most avatars and saints were not all sweetness and light, and some were downright outrageous. For instance, what if you were a moneychanger sitting in your stall at the temple in Jerusalem as your family had done for generations, and suddenly someone overturned your table and whacked you with a whip – would you be inclined to say, "Now there goes an avatar if ever I saw one"?

The most common characteristic I have observed that pertains to all avatars and saints is their ability to transform, empower, and bring out the highest potential of everyone with whom they come in contact.

The following is a list of traits shared by avatars and most divinely inspired people in case you think you may have spotted one. All of them radiated love, kindness, and endless compassion. Some inspired their followers with their wisdom, while others were tireless healers. Some have been known to shock people with outrageous statements and behavior to get their students unstuck. Others displayed psychic abilities to assure us there is more to life than the physical realm, and a few were even revolutionaries.

And there were a few holy people in history who did nothing at all – yet seekers were completely transformed in their presence. Ramana Maharshi, a Hindu saint, was one of those people who could transform someone by just sitting next to them. And his ability to do this is recorded in modern times and on film.

His transmission is not merely a 2000-year-old story that may or may not be true. I know several people who lived on Mt. Arunachala with him, and they assure me he had that kind of presence about him. So keep an eye out for someone displaying any of the above traits.

I suspect most people do not recognize an avatar or a saint when they see them because they have no interest in those qualities. My wise old uncle used to have an expression that summed up that perspective. It went something like this: "when a pickpocket sees a saint, all he sees are the saint's pockets."

As for my teacher, I don't care how anyone describes him. Everyone seemed to see him differently, and usually according to how they viewed themselves. While he often displayed many of the above traits, for many of his students, he was Merlin the Magician on steroids. I describe him as a dragon.

In Daoism, a dragon is not a bad thing. On the contrary, it represents the relentless, powerful yang energy that is necessary to realize one's innate Oneness. It is almost always depicted pursuing the Pearl of Immortality, which is shown as a luminous white ball in front of it. The dragon is a creature that is comfortable in the depths of the Ocean, flying around in the Sky, or walking on the Earth. It is capable of great adaptation and is the guardian of the entrance to the great Oneness.

My teacher not only had many of these dragon qualities, he also seemed to be able to speed up everyone's evolution. If you were in a downward spiral, you went down twice as fast. However, those who stuck with him eventually transformed and learned how to work the spiral.

For instance, if you had an exaggerated fear of death, you would find yourself in a life or death situation twice a week until it was not an issue any more. If you had trouble with rage, you would be triggered hourly. If someone kept falling painfully in and out of love all the time, a new potential soulmate would frequently appear in their lives until they got over that affliction. In his presence, students found that circumstances would arise that forced them to deal with whatever was keeping them from knowing their own wholeness.

When a person is capable of influencing reality like that, we call it being able to co-create their reality. This has nothing to do with the New Age expression, "creating your own reality," which often seems driven by attachment to outcome.

Although he seemed to create his reality, the truth is, he had no strong personal preferences. Misconceptions abound around the idea of our being able to create our own reality, so let's explore that subject a little further before moving along.

Creating your own reality in New Age circles today means little more than the power of positive thinking taken to an extreme. Most people, who are constantly visualizing, or intending, or praying for something, utilize only a small portion of their total being. It is okay to want something and to think positively, but if your desires are not the result of your total being, in harmony with your highest frequency flow, not much will happen.

It is best to remember that only psychotics create their own realities. When highly-evolved people seem to create things, they are simply allowing the Universe to manifest through them. My teacher often said, "If you remain empty, you will receive things and circumstances far beyond anything your conscious mind can conceive of." Of course, it takes many decades of intense cultivation to achieve such emptiness, but that state of being is well worth the effort. So get started.

We're all full of it, which is why we need to cultivate emptiness.

My teacher seemed to know and respect everyone's limits, but he was also capable of breaking those barriers – and he was relentless. He never did anything overt, and you never knew for sure whether he had any hand in your transformation or not. Having known the man for over 22 years and having watched thousands of people change for the better under his influence, I hardly consider their transformations a coincidence. He was a living embodiment of this verse in chapter 17 of the Dao Duh Jing:

A person of Dao works subtly... when they accomplish their task, the people who were benefited will say "We did it ourselves."

A famous classical story from China best describes that method of teaching.

    Once upon a time, a boy was born with a natural talent with the sword. When he was around 13 years of age, his parents pinned a note to his shirt and gave him money to seek out a famous swordsman who they heard lived in the nearby mountains. After months of searching from one cave to another, the boy arrived at the mountain to which everyone pointed as the dwelling place of the sage. As the boy had been properly raised, he did not intrude upon the sage. Instead, he stood in front of the cave until the master came out.

    Eventually, an old man appeared at the entrance and promptly told him to go home. Convinced he had, at last, found the famous swordsman, the boy remained even though the snow was up to his knees. After several more days of rejecting the boy, the master reluctantly admitted he was a swordsman in his youth but insisted he was too old to teach anymore. He also said his reflexes were shot. The boy didn't buy the story and stood his ground. With the snow now up to his waist, the boy was invited inside. After exchanging a few pleasantries, the old man agreed to teach him in the morning.

    The boy was so excited he could not sleep. At dawn, he was in the master's room, swishing his wooden sword around in anticipation of his first lesson. However, the old man said they couldn't work on such a dirty floor and that the boy needed to scrub it. Several days later, when he finished the floor, the master said it was a lousy job and gave him a toothbrush-sized scrubber to use on his next attempt.

Weeks later, the boy finished the job. The master then asked him to bring up water from the valley for them to drink. Because the boy spilled a few drops, he had to repeat the chore until no water was spilled. That took months, and by that time, the master had him cooking his meals and doing his laundry.

At that point, the boy decided the old man was just using him and decided to leave. As he was packing his bag to go, he was hit hard on his head. If it were not for the bump on his head, he thought he might have dreamed it because he was alone in the cave. However, he suspected the master had done it somehow and decided to catch him. He unpacked his bag and began his vigil.

The next day he was hit while cooking, then later while scrubbing the floor, and one time he was even hit while sleeping. Never once did the boy see the master nor hear him coming. By then, he was a mass of bruises and was becoming desperate. Even while sleeping, he stayed intensely alert. A little while later, he was hit and turned so fast he saw the shadow of the master going around the corner. Soon thereafter, he caught a glimpse of his master's robe as he disappeared behind a tree. One day, he turned so fast he actually grabbed the stick out of the master's hand, at which time, the master bowed to him and said his sword training was over.

That boy became the greatest swordsman in the history of China because he could not be hit. His block would go up before the opponent's strike originated. Was the boy taught theory? No. Was he taught techniques? No. Was he talked to at all? No. His intuitions were honed through adverse circumstances until he became a living embodiment of spontaneous response. That was very similar to how I was trained.

First, I was rejected three times. Then I was asked to edit books for years, nonstop. Eventually, unusual circumstances started arising in my life that pushed all my buttons. I had buttons pushed I didn't even know existed! Because my teacher worked 18-hour days, he had a chance to press many constant sources of inspiration for me in the course of a day.

In spite of all my buttons and my inherent laziness, he eventually became convinced of my sincerity and willingness to serve humanity. He then started training me in earnest. After many years of tough "heavenly assignments," as he called them, and 22 years of selfless service to the Daoist cause, I was eventually humiliated and thrown out of his sect!

I called it graduation. Daoists of the Thunder School do not issue caps and gowns. Considering the unnecessary public nature of my expulsion and the fact that I hadn't done anything more horrible than usual, I suspected it was just another test to see if my life would fall apart. Since it didn't, I think he is secretly proud of me. However, many students assured me he had grounds for kicking me out many times over, and they wondered how an arrogant bastard like me actually lasted as long as I did.

After knowing him for several decades and living in the same house with him in Malibu for eight years, and even after his kicking me out of his lineage, I still regard him as being the most mysterious, compassionate, and powerful person I have known. Training with him was like trying to drink from a fire hydrant. He should come with a disclaimer: Beware (be very aware), I am a catalyst for deep change.

Before he returned to Mainland China, he left us with the following – a constant source of inspiration for me.

You are unnamable
While I am nameable.

You are indefinable
While I am definable.

You are immortal
While I am mortal.

You are inexpressible
Yet, I become your expression.

You are unimaginable
Yet, I become your image.

You are formless
Yet, I become your form.

Only when you and I work together
Can the magnificence of the Universe
be displayed.

If you are foolish enough to think this kind of training might be for you, or if you are interested in hearing the details of my 22 years of playing with a dragon – read on.

Chinese	Pinyin	Meaning
長	Chang	(long)
心	Hsin	(heart)
或	Huo	(perhaps)
退	T'ui	(to withdraw)
和	Ho	(amicable)
知	Chih	(to know)
鈿	T'ien	(silver filigree)
細	Hsi	(thin)
北	Pei	(North)
風	Feng	(wind)
外	Wai	(outside)
飛	Fei	(fly)
内	Nei	(interior)
好	Hao	(good)
門	Men	(door)
幼	Yu	(young)
助	Chu	(to help)
幼	Yu	(young)
即	Chi	(immediately)
部	Pu	(department)
家	Chia	(home)
官	Kuan	(officer)
空	K'ung	(empty)
宥	Yu	(to pardon)

EDITING WITH MY DAOIST TEACHER

Meanwhile, back at my teacher's clinic in Taiwan, my friends were as impressed with him as I was. We agreed to help him translate and edit his sacred books into English if he would tutor us in acupuncture. For the next couple of months, we went to his home early every day and stayed until after dark.

After a few days of editing his translations, it became apparent to us that our teacher's unusual English was the result of his photographic memory combined with very little contact with English-speaking people. While he had memorized much of his English dictionary, he did not know when and how to use certain words or even which words or expressions we no longer use.

One day he said, "Sit in my new, ah... the word is on page 1,062 upper right corner, and it starts with an s."

"Sofa," I quickly guessed. "No." he said. "The word is settee." I went to that page, and the word was settee. "We don't use that word anymore," I told him. So he asked me to put a check mark before all the words we no longer use. Until then, I had no idea how many words in our dictionary had become outdated, not to mention how irrational and tense-bound English is for Chinese-speaking people.

After a few months of helping him, I ran out of money. To pay expenses, I taught English conversation to local folks. It was then I fully realized just how difficult English is for the Chinese, who are used to reading pictograms instead of phonetic letters. Can you imagine having to vocalize and make sense of these sentences?

The bandage was wound around the wound.

The dump was so full, they had to refuse more refuse.

The soldier decided to desert his companions in the desert.

The insurance was invalid for the invalid.

He was too close to the door to close it.

And try explaining this sentence:

All the faith he had had had no effect on his life.

Our teacher often said, "It is no wonder you English-speaking people are so tense. It is because you have so many tenses in your language."

Chinese has no tenses. They say, "Tomorrow I do" or "Today I do" or "Yesterday I do." Whereas English speakers say, "I do," "I did," "I have done," and so on. Our language has an insidious tendency to break up the stream of timelessness into non-existent pieces, thereby rendering most of us time-bound and overly tensed.

He would also say, "There can be no hope for a civilization that writes like crabs walk." (Sideways; the Chinese used to write from top to bottom and from right to left, but they changed recently by writing in the same direction we do.) I believe that learning a language that is pictorial instead of phonetic, and reading vertically instead of horizontally, increases one's intelligence. Anyone who has been involved with IQ tests taken by people from different countries knows that Asians generally do better than Caucasians. How does an English-speaking person like me answer questions like this: "Teacher Mark, why is the word big smaller than the word small, and why is the word abbreviated so long?"

Translating literally from Chinese to English is impossible. Our words and their characters have multiple levels of meaning; to make matters worse, their characters often imply things and ideas, whereas we have three or four words with nearly the same meaning.

One of the most humorous and clear examples of the fallacy of trying to translate verbatim came to me while walking one fine day in downtown Gau Shung (my phonetic spelling of Kao Hsung, the city where we lived in Taiwan). On a theater marquee, I saw a crude sign written in English that read: "Famous American movie inside." I investigated and found out the title of the movie was *Violin Player on the Ceiling*. Since I had never heard of that movie, I decided to investigate further. Eventually, I realized that someone had translated the three Chinese characters they were given from their Chinese/English dictionary and their resulting translation turned out to be a far cry from *Fiddler on the Roof!*

While I am on the subject of language, I must point out that most languages make Play exceedingly difficult unless one is a poet. However, since English is primarily a noun-based language, which results in subject-verb-object constructions, it leads to a worldview in which subjects and objects are separate things that require conjoining.

In verb-based languages, subject and object are implicit in the verb, which is sufficient to convey meaning.

For instance, in English, we say, "It is raining." What in hell is the "it" and what is an "is?" A person using a verb-based language would simply go outside and say, "raining" and probably start spontaneously jumping around in it. How can we ever hope to directly experience the timeless nature of reality when our every word is dissecting the flow of life into past and future perfect tenses? This pathetic attempt to order and control our lives creates a sense of separation that impedes the natural spontaneity that is a foundation of a Playful life. The tragedy of subject-object language is this: Not only does it construct our reality largely by limiting what we think, it also determines the way we think!

Think about it.

Dragon's Play in Taiwan

After working with my teacher for a few weeks, I became aware of his other unusual gifts and powers.

He eventually invited us to join him and his local students at their Sunday morning service on their third floor.

Every week they meditated, read from his sacred books, and asked questions about Daoism. Occasionally, unusual phenomena happened. One Sunday morning, a student fell to the floor then jumped up to proclaim he was an ancient Daoist shaman.

He invited us to ask him questions. After hearing many of what I thought were really dumb questions like, "When will I meet my future bride?" or "Who was I in my last life?" the "shaman" said something like, "I came back after 4,000 years to answer these stupid questions? I am outta here!" The student then came out of the trance and wondered why everyone was staring at him.

According to other students, that kind of psychic phenomenon frequently occurred in the presence of my teacher. Having seen a lot of that kind of stuff before, I was more impressed that someone other than myself thought those questions were stupid. Too bad I had to find somebody who was "4,000 years old" who finally agreed with me about something.

My uncle had a spirit who used to speak through him all the time – especially after he had been drinking. His ancient friend said he was 40,000 years old and claimed he was the younger brother of Ramtha (the spirit entity channeled by American mystic and author JZ Knight). Unfortunately, my uncle's spirit-friend had a lisp, stuttered, and spoke with a heavy accent that was impossible to understand.

Another strange incident occurred when I found an ancient sword used in exorcisms. I tried to pull it out of its sheath, but it was rusted shut. "Don't fool around with it. It has a lot of inherent power that could be dangerous to you," my teacher warned. I didn't believe him and kept trying to pull it out. Eventually, he said he would do it to prevent me from hurting myself.

Before continuing this story, you must know of the fat rat in his house that often ran across the rafters. My teacher called him the Mayor of Gau Shung. When my teacher pulled on the sword with great force, it ended up pointing to the rafter where the rat was sitting – and down fell the Mayor with a thud! Dead. (Three of us witnessed it.) Even though my teacher later cultivated the power of exorcism in me, he never gave me that sword. I can't help but think this had something to do with the cautionary tale told in the Disney movie, *The Sorcerer's Apprentice.*

Another time, while we sat around talking, a big old turtle crawled out from under my chair. "What the hell is that?" I said with a start. "He is an old, immortal friend of mine, and how he came to me is an interesting story," my teacher explained.

Whenever he said something was interesting, I usually ended up saying something like, "Wow!"

One day the postal worker brought him a box containing the turtle and a letter from a Taipei construction worker who was digging a foundation for an office building. About 12 feet underground, his shovel hit a hard object, which turned out to be the turtle. He and his fellow workers were astounded the turtle was alive. He took it home, and that night had a dream in which the spirit of the turtle appeared and instructed him to mail himself to his Daoist friend in Gau Shung. Since my teacher was known throughout the city, he was not hard to find. From that time on, I viewed that turtle with more respect.

My friends and I continued translating, editing, and studying acupuncture with him until we got the nerve to ask him to come to America. To our surprise, he said yes. We also asked for initiation into his sect, and again he said yes, even though a foreigner had never before been allowed to join. I wondered at the time why he didn't deny us three times before initiating us as the books said he should. It wasn't until I returned to the US that I found out he had no intention of skipping that little detail!

For our initiation ceremony, he chose an astrologically auspicious time – 2 a.m. on a Friday. Why can't those sacred moments occur at 4 or 5 p.m. just before happy hour? Anyhow, just before it started, he said my pants were too dirty and gave me another pair to wear. They were...drum roll...three sizes too large for me, so I did the entire ceremony holding them up with my left hand. I surmised he was telling me I had big pants to fill.

The actual ceremony was simple, direct, and powerful. After lighting the incense and candles and arranging the flowers, we purified ourselves with a fire and water ritual. We first passed a flame over our heads and around our bodies, then sprinkled ourselves with water. We read our letter of intent and then approached the shrine on our knees with the letter of petition on top of our heads. He then touched us on top of our heads. (That was the powerful part.) We then bowed to him and to his students who were there to witness our ceremony. We also bowed to his altar, which held objects that belonged to people from his spiritual lineage. It actually felt like they were in the room with us. That was it – nothing spectacular, except I walked around in a transcendent state for several days because of that touch.

After the ceremony, a long-time student of his told me that several weeks before we three arrived, he announced that "ambassadors" from the United States were coming to visit, and he would soon be leaving with them. He assured his students that being with him for 26 years was a good foundation for their lives, and now they must learn to get along without him. The student also told me our teacher went out and bought three new chairs just before we arrived.

THE DRAGON COMES TO MALIBU

Soon after our initiation in mid-1975, we returned to the United States to prepare a center for our teacher. My traveling companions had a home in the Malibu hills, so we converted their multi-level house into an acupuncture clinic and shrine. We had to wait a few months for him to join us because he had trouble convincing his wife and two boys it was a good idea to move to the US. Eventually, all the arrangements were made, and I must say, his departure from Taiwan made the story of my planned move to Darwin look like a minor incident.

He was scheduled to fly from Gau Shung to Taipei in August to visit friends there. Then three days later, he was to fly to Los Angeles. His wife and boys were to remain there for a few weeks to settle some matters and then join him several weeks later.

On the day he was scheduled to leave Gau Shung, a super typhoon (Nina, the worst storm in recorded history in that area) hit the city and seriously damaged it. We were unable to get through on the telephone for several days. We finally reached his wife, who said there was so much damage to the city and airport, a student of his had to arrange a military aircraft to get him out. (My teacher had been a bodyguard for Chiang Kai-shek and still had military connections.)

His wife also said the streets were so littered with debris that no one could drive in them. Their house, which they had just sold, was seriously damaged. The roof was torn up, and the third floor where they had their shrine was gutted. Nothing like that had happened in more than the 20 years they were in that house. The building next door where the shrine implements were placed on the roof with only a tarp over them was untouched.

By shrine implements, I don't mean a candle and a statue of Jesus on the cross...I am talking about 3,000 years of his family's inheritance! His family was among the earliest Daoists to spread Qigong to many towns and cities in China. Some of those historical artifacts included priceless old statues of the "3 Pure Ones" and fragile bamboo strips that included the writings of many famous Daoists. All the more amazing they survived undamaged!

After speaking with our teacher's wife, we breathed easily until we turned on the TV the next night and saw the Taipei airport runway torn up by that same powerful storm. Apparently, the storm headed north and slammed into Taipei the same day he was to leave there. We got through on the telephone immediately and found out from his friends that he had caught the last plane out before the airport was shut down. Even the air traffic control tower was destroyed. Then the storm headed into the mainland and did a lot of damage there.

"What was that all about?" I asked upon meeting him at the Los Angeles Airport. "The forces of darkness were trying to stop my influence in the world, but they had no chance," he responded in his usual, understated tone.

Then the real training began. Shortly after his arrival in the US, he kicked me out. He frightened my girlfriend away by acting as if he idolized her. Then he told me her leaving was my fault. The next thing I knew I was sitting in my old apartment in North Hollywood near the Taoist sanctuary, wondering what had happened.

At first, I was relieved to be away from him, but a thought kept nagging me. This was not his typical behavior, so what was really going on? I took great pride in my intuitions about people and figured there must be a lesson for me in all this. It soon occurred to me he had been acting out a caricature of my tendency to put women I love on a pedestal and practically worship them. The next day I got a phone call from the center with the following message: "Rumor has it that if you crawl back to him on your hands and knees, he will take you back." Little did I know they meant it literally.

There I was a few days later, on my knees, with a letter of petition on top of my head, just like in our initiation ceremony. Only, this time, I promised to be a good boy and expressed my understanding that I was on probation. This meant I had to sit in the back of the assembly room and keep my mouth shut.

Years later, it occurred to me that all the fuss over my ex-girlfriend was his way of showing me my relationships with women in particular, and people in general, were unbalanced. I either scorned the ones I didn't like or idealized those I liked. These two extremes had to go if I ever hoped to relate to others in a meaningful way. I am still working on that one. Things went well for a few weeks until he accused me of taking advantage of an attractive woman I was working with in the clinic. Even though I hadn't done anything unethical, I found myself back in another apartment in the same complex in North Hollywood – my second expulsion.

I eventually did admit that if she hadn't been so attractive, I would not have given her so much attention. He let me return for honestly facing my motives. For weeks, I was assigned all the alcoholics and drug addicts to work with to test my resolve to serve everyone regardless of how physically or psychologically unattractive I found them. The lesson was learned. Even when I opened my own clinic years later, I never refused a patient.

My third expulsion dealt with my next obstacle to a life of Play – arrogance. A few weeks after my second triumphant return, in one of his Sunday morning services where I was supposed to keep my mouth shut, I broke probation by asserting myself with a solution to one of his koans. A koan is a riddle that is intellectually unsolvable, yet you have to creatively solve it. (Contrary to what you may have heard, the Zen Buddhists adopted koan training from the Daoists because Zen Buddhism originated as a result of the interface between those two great religions.)

A typical Zen Buddhist koan might be phrased like this, "What was the shape of your face before your parents were born?" If you take paradoxical puzzles seriously, they can push you beyond rational thought into a transcendent state. For example, the above koan forces you to see beyond the world of dualism that your father and mother represent, into a pre-existent state of transcendent unity represented by your face before they were born.

Now, just saying that to a master will not be a correct answer. You must present that state of unity consciousness directly to the master, or you might get whacked with a stick! Your response would only be accepted after you did or said something authentically spontaneous.

Meanwhile, I sat quietly at the back of his gatherings for what seemed like an eternity (probably weeks!), listening to some of the dumbest responses to his koans imaginable. Since I had read several books on koans and how to respond to them, I could no longer stifle my impatience. I stood up and put my shoe on my head, indicating I understood it.

And he said, "Yes, that's it. You are out of here again." Even though I went into a state of complete spontaneity because I had no forethought as to what I would do or say, he obviously saw this and "rewarded" me by kicking me out again!

I would still be sitting in that North Hollywood complex, where they now knew me on a first-name basis, if his students hadn't asked the *E Jing* repeatedly who should get my old room. Consistently it indicated that room belonged to me. Since no one in Daoism argues with the *E Jing*, I got it back – seemingly to my teacher's chagrin.

A year later, I realized those three expulsions were my three denials because he never did anything like that again for 22 years. If he had denied me initiation in Taiwan when I expected that response, it would have meant nothing. But for him to bring me into the inner circle and then kick me out three times, that really tested my resolve to learn and grow under his tutelage. Most religions seek converts, but high-level Daoists reject you to test your sincerity.

As soon as I stopped getting kicked out, I was able to settle down and do some serious editing. We cranked out eight books in eight years, several of which have become standards in the field. All the while, I was watching wave after wave of eager students coming and going through our center and not staying long enough to learn anything. My teacher even had a name for them: "meteorites." They burn brightly for a short time, and then they are gone.

To make matters worse, my teacher seemed to encourage people to leave. One of his little tricks was to not talk much during his Tai Ji classes.

I couldn't understand why, so I asked. "Are you aware you just lost 50 percent of your students in that Tai Ji class because you don't talk to them?" "Good," he replied, "my plan is working. Tai Ji takes a lot of practice and patience to get good at it, and if they need me to change their emotional diapers every day, they will never do it on their own. Let them go to a teacher who will tell them what beautiful souls they are."

I must admit that most of those students were later shown to be undisciplined, impulsive, self-indulgent, spoiled brats for the most part. Instant gratification with little effort and an endless appetite for feeling good seemed to be their driving motivation. As a result, they missed the opportunity to learn Daoist wisdom.

Playing in Malibu

We didn't just study Tai Ji with my teacher. Those who stayed and made the effort benefited from a variety of Daoist cultivations. I use the word cultivations because I think it most accurately describes our daily routines. Most religions emphasize faith, prayer, chanting, or song, but we Daoists regard our spirits as being like young trees. Give trees enough water, sunshine, and rich soil, and they will grow strong on their own – just as we will when properly nourished. Most Daoist masters often refer to themselves as gardeners.

Speaking of trees, the first thing our teacher had us do after his arrival was to meditate in the tops of the evergreen trees growing in the backyard. He claimed we needed this because we were all too restless and aggressive. I hoisted a small chair up near the top of a tree, and made myself as comfortable as possible. I hear the chair is still there. The energy up there is quite calming. Try it if you suffer from mental restlessness.

Next, he introduced his Eight Treasures Chi Gung style to us. I referred to the Eight Treasures as the Roto-Rooter of the meridian system, which are the energy channels of the body used in acupuncture. I still regard the Eight Treasures as one of the more physically demanding and complex energetic styles available today. I have seen quite a few styles, having judged over 50 Tai Ji tournaments in the past 25 years.

His decision to teach that style surprised me because he was known for his fighting ability. I expected him to teach us Gung Fu. However, he said that because of our aggressiveness, he didn't want to encourage any more of it. If we practiced this style diligently, he promised it could save us from the "L" we were living in.

I told him, "The word you are trying to pronounce is hell." He said, "No, I mean the letter 'L'."

He described how many of us go through our entire day with our bodies frozen in the unnatural shape of an "L." The first thing we do upon waking is to slump on the edge of our beds in that position. Even our arms and bodies are in the shape of an "L." We then take a few steps to the kitchen table, where we sit in the "L" eating crappy food. A few more steps and we're sitting in our cars with our arms and body in the same position. In front of our computers at work, we manage to stay in that unhealthy position for nearly eight hours. Then it's time for another "L" of a car ride home where we load up on 2,000 more calories we don't need. Most of us then waddle off to the couch with our remotes in our hands for a long evening in the "L" position. His solution to the "L" was the "I" position, whether as a standing meditation or as Tai Ji.

The original Eight Treasures he taught us were designed as a gross solution for gross blockages. He would not allow us to do it within the same day of practicing Tai Ji because of the differences in frequency. We did that style for nearly a year before we resumed with his more subtle Earth style of Chi Gung/Tai Ji.

Another cultivation we would do every morning was to march single file to the top of the Malibu hills to absorb the energy of the Sun rising. Sometimes we would experience the full Moon setting in the West at the same time, so we would absorb the energy of each heavenly body through our palms simultaneously. Wow. It was almost like sticking our fingers into two bare light sockets at the same time while standing ankle-deep in a puddle of water.

We also read incantations and meditated in different standing and sitting positions. We even had a sleeping posture that stimulated acupuncture points on the right side of our brains (the creative/intuitive side of the brain). We were in a meditative state every second of the day and night, regardless of what we were doing.

Every 60 days, we would meditate all night long to absorb the double "metal energy day" of the Chinese energy calendar. It is thought that the metal energy is the energy of reformation, which he obviously thought we all needed at the time. On one of those nights, he asked if any of us thought we could stand holding a single stick of incense without moving until it burned out. Several of us volunteered, and out he came from his herb room with several four-foot-long sticks of incense that took eight hours to burn! I am proud to say that I was the only one who stood un-moving for the entire eight hours – though I kind of cheated. After four hours, I dissolved into the Void, and the chi held me up effortlessly the rest of the time. It didn't happen due to any intention on my part. It just happened spontaneously, or I would not have been able to do it.

He also had us do a cultivation called self-release. It was very similar to the chaotic meditation done by the Hindus. The only difference between the two was that he mumbled some Daoist incantations over our heads, and as a result, the experience was twice as powerful. This type of meditation encourages spontaneous movement, and some people even ended up writhing on the floor.

Others growled like animals, some threw up, but most people just went outside where things were normal. Once again, I never moved.

After a while, some of my most respected friends said I must be one of the most inhibited and blocked individuals they ever met. I went to my teacher and asked, "I think I am just clear. Who is right?" He said, "You are both right. You are clear and one of the most blocked people I know." I thought I would die laughing at that response. We Daoists revel in contradictions.

In other people's chaotic meditation classes, I have noticed that all students start swaying, as if that is the goal. Actually, the idea is to be a clear conduit of energy, no matter how powerful the surge. Some movement is the creative process in action, but most of it is caused by blocked chi trying to flow through the body. Psychological imbalances can also trigger movements, especially spasms. The goal of this cultivation is a smooth flow of chi, whether you are moving or not.

It was around this time I learned that the phenomenon of "poisonous palms" is not just an exaggerated tall tale. I had heard many stories about old Tai Ji masters debilitating or outright killing people with a touch, but I didn't take them seriously. Now I am a believer, based on my own personal experience. I take no one's word for anything. I question everything. You can avoid a lot of mythical/fantasy nonsense with that attitude, and most of my experiences are repeatable – although I chose not to repeat this one.

One day before our Tai Ji class, our teacher asked us to try pushing him down. Of course, no one could do it. When it came my turn to try, I decided not to go easy on him and that I would quickly knock him on his ass before he knew what hit him. Since I have cat-like reflexes and had done a little boxing while living in Pittsburgh, I was confident I could do it.

He seemed to sense what I had in mind when he said, "If you have any notion of succeeding, I want you to know you are not even in my league, so don't even try." With one finger, he lightly touched me on the right side of my chest and walked away with a smirk on his face.

I wondered what he was smiling about until the shock wore off, and the pain began. Have you ever had a Charley horse cramp or muscle spasm? Imagine five muscles cramping up at the same time and in the same location, and you might have a sense of what I was experiencing. I rolled around on the ground, clutching my swollen chest, trying to scream. He returned to assure me he only put his finger on "stun," so there would be no serious consequences. Thank God for small favors. An hour later, I had to turn the ignition key in my car with my left hand because my right arm was still useless.

Later, he admitted that stories about masters killing tigers on another mountain by pointing at them were highly exaggerated. He told me only he and one other person he ever met had that kind of training and power. He insisted that close physical contact is necessary. Rest assured, you cannot be killed by a martial artist pointing his finger at you from a distance. Of course, pointing your middle finger up at someone else might get you killed, so be careful about that.

It was also during the first two years of training he grew "tonsils" on my elbows. This was after I casually let it be known that I had my tonsils removed when I was a kid. Horrified, he said, "Our tonsils, like our appendix, are like a red signal light that flashes when things are getting too toxic in our bodies." He asked me, "If we take those signaling devices out of our bodies, how do we know when we are getting overly toxic?"

Of course, I had no answer. He said not to worry; he would grow new tonsils for me. I thought he was going to grow them in my throat, but he started a fire on my elbows! He put a piece of ginger on an acupuncture point at Large Intestine #11, which is located at each elbow. He then put a small pile of moxa (an herb that burns) on them and lit them! They burned down into those spots and hurt like hell.

That pleasant little procedure raised two white welts a quarter of an inch high, which lasted for years. He said he would have to renew them every few years. Needless to say, I politely declined.

Sure enough, whenever I pigged out on sweets around Christmas time, my new "tonsils" glowed red for a few days until I fasted. He explained that removing our tonsils is almost as ridiculous as driving while a red light is flashing on the dashboard, and then what do we do about it? We pull over to the side of the road and smash the red light!

Around the third year, he came to me and said that having the power of exorcism would be useful to me in the future, so I consented to learn it. Once again, I didn't know what I was getting myself into. My preparation and training turned out to be 49 days of fasting with nightlong incantations invoking the power of the deities of the Big Dipper.

The most difficult part was that I wasn't allowed to have sex during that time. He always insisted that if I would simply remain celibate, I would live forever. Well, what I discovered is that you don't really live forever – it just seems like forever! I was celibate for 16 years once, but the minute I turned 17, I said enough of that nonsense.

The Daoists don't hold up a cross and hope for the best when doing an exorcism. They are quite scientific about it. They maintain that the configuration of the veins in the upper eyeball, which are normally out of sight, will change according to the kind of spirit doing the possessing. My first duty was to roll back the upper eyelids on the poor wretch who was screaming obscenities and projectile vomiting green slime all over me. (As you might guess, I have seen *The Exorcist*.) After checking out a person's veins, I refer to a chart of vein configurations to know what kind of spirit I was dealing with.

There are all kinds of different spirits, and one must learn how to communicate with them. Not all spirits are evil. Some are justified in raising a little hell with some people, so it is important to know how to interact with them.

What if you unknowingly build a house on a sacred burial site and anger the spirits there? Negotiation and compromise are often possible. If not, I have the power and techniques to destroy any invading nasty spirit. "Who ya gonna call?" (As in *Ghostbusters*.)

The night I graduated from that training, I was having dinner in a restaurant with a friend, and a friend of hers came up to our table and asked if she knew anyone who was an exorcist! She became my first client, but she turned out not to be possessed – she was just crazier than hell. I gave her an amulet to tie around her ankle, and from that moment, she had no more problems with invading spirits.

I have been called to do an exorcism only two other times in 30 years. Neither time did I find the individuals possessed. I suspect that in our modern age of disbelief in such things, anyone who might be possessed is in a nut house or running for political office. My teacher once mentioned that a person couldn't be possessed unless they are already in a weakened or imbalanced state. So stay healthy, balanced, and wise, and you will have nothing to worry about.

Although my teacher hired himself out as an exorcist, a rain-maker, and a spiritualist medium in his younger days in Mainland China, he didn't do much of that in the United States. However, one day just before I left our Malibu center to teach around the country, he went into trance: it was quite unusual, even for me. We gathered a group of about ten students for a Chi Gung workshop, but all of a sudden, he announced a dead friend of his wanted to speak to us through him. My master said, "There is one little problem. My friend now lives inside the Sun, and it is too cold in this room for him. Start a fire and bring me some blankets."

The room was already 85 degrees Fahrenheit before we closed the windows and built a big fire in the wood stove. Around 120 degrees, we were all drenched in sweat and ready to run out of the room when he announced he wanted more blankets! About 15 blankets later, he spoke with a different personality who was busily describing everyone's five-element energy composition. My teacher's friend must have been an astute observer of people when he lived on the Earth because from what I knew about the students in the room, he was accurate in his assessment of them.

Regardless of how interesting the spirit was, we kept thanking him for coming because we all wanted out of that room! He finally got the hint we wanted him to leave, so he started getting snippy. He said, "I am going now, and I don't need your thanks." I snipped back, "We people down here on Planet Earth don't need 15 blankets to talk to each other."

I wasn't going to take any crap from someone just because he chose to live in the Sun, and besides, that is a stupid place to hang out anyway. The fascinating thing behind all that theater was the fact that when my teacher was speaking as the other person, he did not sweat under all those blankets. When he later started speaking as himself, the sweat shot out of his body, and he nearly trampled us, getting out of that room as fast as he could.

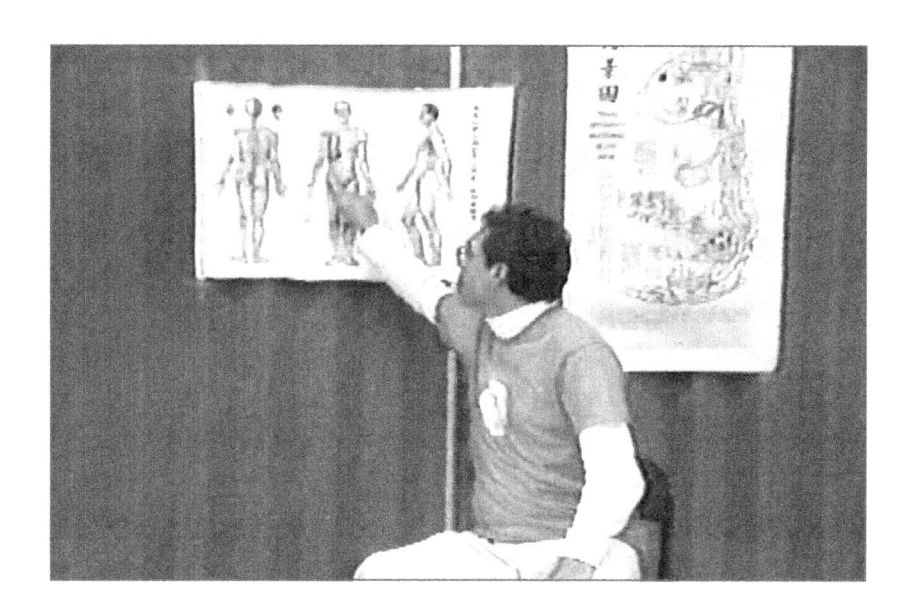

Learning While Teaching

After I spent nearly five years doing one weird cultivation after another, my teacher announced the next phase in my evolution was to broaden my focus by helping others through teaching.

"Your days of boot camp for enlightenment and beyond are over," he said. For the next hour, he conveyed to me the seriousness of this life transition. "Your life is not your own. This spiritual path is not about freeing yourself from suffering and securing your own happiness, regardless of what you learned from the Buddhists. It is about participating in something far greater."

He explained that I am accountable to everyone for everything I do. Once I realized that he said, I would no longer have time for my petty concerns. I would discover my actions have profound consequences far beyond myself.

"Challenges will continue," he said, "but they will seem less significant, and you will find that your freedom from self-concern will be contagious." He told me to get out there and teach this stuff.

Once again, my life took a dramatic turn from what I had expected. At first, I was hesitant to teach, even though a few years earlier, I had been ready to be the Messiah of the modern age. I must have gained some humility along the way because I didn't feel qualified to teach his advanced practices. Don't get the idea I am humble now – even miracles have their limits!

More than that, I felt hypocritical teaching spiritual matters. I felt like a person composed of saltwater sitting at the edge of the ocean selling saltwater to beings also made up of saltwater. Why should I, or anyone, encourage a longing for spiritual experiences when everyone is already spiritual by nature? The whole process seemed to draw out people's discontent with themselves. Left to their own devices, they would eventually have their own spiritual experiences even though it might take several thousand lifetimes to accomplish it.

My teacher agreed that people can sometimes have spiritual experiences by accident, but it was my job to make them "accident-prone." He also agreed that the winds of grace are always blowing, but we must learn how to raise our sails to catch it. He assured me that the only way I would really learn this stuff was to teach it and that I would learn a lot from my students. With that encouragement, I launched wholeheartedly into my new career as a wandering Daoist mentor.

First, I noticed how effective my teacher's advanced practices were in comparison to others, and the reason was because of how well integrated they were. Each practice had elements of the others within it, and they all contributed to the three-tiered spiritual structure.

1. The foundation of the structure is the physical body. For most people, this is the only body they are aware of, and yet, you would be surprised how many people are not

connected to their bodies. They have no knowledge of it, very little control over it, and they certainly do not treat it as a manifestation of spirit.

2. The second is the bioelectrical body. Very few people are aware of this aspect of their being. This energetic body is composed of the energy that flows through the meridians that acupuncture and Chi Gung work with.

3. The third is the subtle, extended auric body. Many religions depict this body as a halo around a person's head. Actually, auras extend around the entirety of every physical body. You don't need to be holy to have an aura or to be able to see one.

Comprehensive health involves the harmonious integration of those three bodies. Each body must be in balance and in clear communication with the others. To be in balance requires continuous balancing because none of our three bodies is static. Anything in excess (including too much moderation) disrupts the balance and becomes the basis of "dis-ease."

Any one of our three bodies can show the first signs of a problem. For example, a spiritual crisis or a crisis of meaning will first be seen in the auric body – by those who have been trained to see it. That high-frequency auric energy field will immediately interact with the meridian system and can energize and heal most symptoms at that frequency. Of course, if you lose a leg in a car crash, call an ambulance! Dealing with the purely physical is western medicine at its best.

However, if you catch a problem while it is only manifesting at a psychological or spiritual frequency, you can save yourself a lot of trouble by going to a highly trained acupuncturist. If you don't believe me, go to the doctor's office and tell him you have an auric problem and see what they say.

Emotional difficulties first affect the meridian system. For instance, intense fear can stop the chi flow through the bladder and kidneys. If you don't get the bioelectrical flow going in those areas of your body in a hurry, you will end up soiling your jeans. If a large metal object hits you, all three bodies will be seriously affected at roughly the same time.

Another way to look at our three bodies is to liken them to the three phases of H2O – ice, water, and steam. Because H2O can vibrate at different frequencies, it transitions through those three phases. Likewise, according to the Daoists, humans can experience their different energetic bodies by identifying with their different frequencies.

Our physical bodies correspond to the ice-cube phase of H2O and share the world of dense, hard objects – unable to physically penetrate each other – except for sex, of course. Our fluid, bioelectrical bodies resemble the water stage because our electrical bodies can interpenetrate each other to some extent. (See the chapter on Daoist sexuality.) Our auric bodies are similar to the steam phase in that they are subtle, far-reaching, and invisible to most people. Steam is invisible. It is the condensation around the steam that everyone sees. Our auric bodies can interpenetrate all of the other grosser bodies just mentioned.

If you are only aware of your physical body, you are out of touch with two-thirds of your being. Our present allopathic sick-care system needs to involve all three bodies in its diagnosis and treatments. Otherwise, it will continue to be incomplete and ineffective when dealing with systemic problems. The allopathic method mostly treats symptoms and usually with powerful drugs – seldom getting to the deep underlying psychological and spiritual causes.

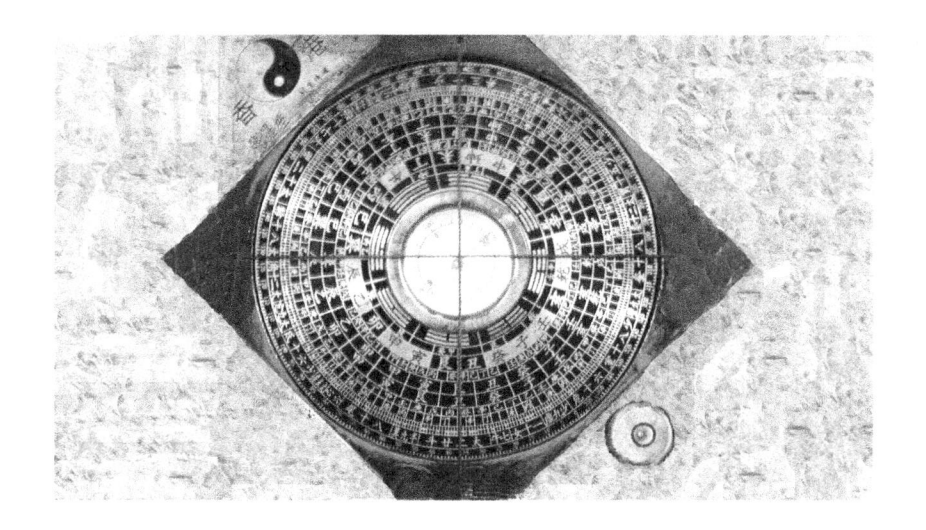

Teaching Popular Feng Shui

One of the first workshops I taught was Feng Shui because I had been doing it since 1975. I will not go into too much detail since I am not as enamored with it as I used to be. Instead, I will clue you into a few differences among the various schools as practiced in the United States. That way, if you decide to hire someone to evaluate your environment, which often includes your own personal energy composition, you will know which school does what. Currently, the most popular schools in the United States are the BTB (Black Tantric Buddhist) School, the Eight Directions or East/ West Compass School, and the Flying Stars Compass Schools. All three use different methods to evaluate an office, home, or gravesite.

I have watched the various schools for decades now, and at present, they all seem to promise more than they deliver. I realize how lucky I was to study the Eight Directions Compass School first because I now regard it as the middle of the road school compared to the two extremes. It is primarily concerned with the energy composition of the house, everyone in it, and how to harmonize it all.

The energy of the house is mostly determined by its facing direction. The energy of the people in it is determined by an energy calendar that has been around for thousands of years. The year of someone's birth determines their energy composition, and that calendar gives the energy of the year, month, day, and hour. Hence, it is called the four pillars of destiny. From it, you can learn what your strengths and weaknesses are and perhaps find a home that can compensate for any imbalances. If not, many instructors will offer "remedies" that can be used to create harmony.

I taught the East/West Compass School for over ten years until I began to suspect the five-element energy calendar that all the Compass Schools relied on (as does Chinese Astrology) was no longer in sync with the planet's real energies. So I decided to look at what the other schools were doing.

The first school I investigated was the BTB School because it had just arrived in the United States and was spreading like wildfire. It was introduced by Lin Yun, who was heavily influenced by Tibetan Buddhist shamanism. As a result, their practices are 80% shamanistic spiritual practices and 20% classic feng shui. They have door-guarding rituals, evil-energy repelling practices (called mudras), and cures for every affliction. Unfortunately, they do not take into consideration the energy composition of the occupants nor the direction the house is facing, which are critical and fundamental to the Compass Schools. I concluded his methods simplify Feng Shui to the point of it not even being Feng Shui.

I studied the Flying Star Schools (Xuan Kong) even though I was still suspicious of their energy calendar. I was intrigued by them bringing in more dimensions than other schools, such as the age of the house – which they need to know to determine in which of the nine 20-year cycles it was built. They surmise that every 20 years,

ALL houses change their energy arrangements, and remedies dispersed in certain rooms must be re-shuffled. Their New Year's Day in 2024 is the next big shake up so watch for your local Flying Star practitioner scrambling around their house on that date, repainting, moving furniture, and re-dispersing remedies. All that fuss because they think a new, five-element energy will move into the center spot, changing everything.

I quickly concluded that piling up a bunch of mostly incompatible five-phase energies in all areas of a house was no way to harmonize with the environment. The Flying Star School was complicated beyond belief, so I did not teach it. Though I am convinced the energy calendar used by the various Compass Schools is no longer accurate, I applaud the Chinese for creating an energy calendar in the first place. The energetic foundation is valid. It is just that every new emperor started that 60-unit energy cycle at the beginning of his reign. Finally, in 1911, Sun Yat-sen reset the calendar to begin at the start of the reign of the Yellow Emperor, a semi-mythical figure. The Yellow Emperor's reign was so far back in antiquity no one knows exactly when he lived. How capricious can you be in determining the start of a 60-unit energetic cycle that purportedly holds the fate of everyone and everything?

When I realized the contradiction, I interviewed practitioners of all the major schools, asking each of them the same question. "Why did you choose your particular school?" The replies were the same: "Our method is the most effective." That answer tells me we need serious scientific investigation into Feng Shui. No doubt, we and our environment on this planet are influenced by cosmic cycles. But now, we have the technological capability to accurately determine what energies are influencing us the most, and when and how they operate. So, now let's use our modern tools to better understand this ancient science!

I have no doubt that people trying to harmonize their homes will be successful to some extent, if only because of their focused intent and the power of suggestion.

My suspicion about that calendar is the least of my Feng Shui concerns. The ignorance and fanaticism I have observed over the years worries me most. I am not just referring to the clientele but also to the practitioners!

I knew a practitioner of the Flying Star School who calculated she needed the fire energy in the southwest corner of her house. That area happened to be the bathroom. So, she put the family TV (sometimes used as a fire energy remedy) in that area, and the only place it would fit was on the toilet. I am sure her family would still be enjoying their favorite evening programs if it were not for her kids complaining about the cold, hard tiles hurting their little butts.

One aspect of Feng Shui I do not hesitate to recommend is how to create a shrine in your home. Having a quiet place to retreat to daily is as important to your psyche as having wilderness places to visit in your environment. Nearly everyone recognizes the benefit of taking a little time every day to let our minds and emotions calm down.

Here is how the Daoists make a shrine. Construct it away from the heavily trafficked areas of your home. Be creative with it. Put in things of value to you. Build it in three tiers. The bottom level holds all the sacred implements representing the material realm: A water vessel; a place for a candle to light up your day; an incense holder, etc. The second level is reserved for pictures and/or books of the holy ones we hold dear. This level encourages togetherness and compassion – the human realm. The top level is for something that reminds us of transcendence, the state of being one with all that is. Many use the Buddhist circle. The Daoists put the *E Jing* on the top shelf. My Christian friends put the cross up there, etc. Do try this at home!

Teaching Natural Feng Shui

In contrast to my cautionary attitude, my Chinese teacher revived my interest in it with a casual remark he once made that took Feng Shui to a higher level for me. He said: "Certain environments encourage particular psyches, and they, in time, create different philosophies and religions."

For instance, have you noticed that cold climate people are more aggressive than those who live in warmer climates? Did Europe stand a chance against the Vikings? Did South America fare well against the Europeans? How did the Han Chinese or anybody do against the Mongols? (Does the name Genghis Khan ring a bell?) And can you imagine what the poor Dravidians in India must have gone through when the cold climate Aryans over-ran them a long time ago and imposed the caste system on them? And, of course, the Aryans set themselves up as the Brahmins and ran the show for a long time.

Another observation I noticed that confirms what my teacher alluded to is the fact that before the influence of mass media, people who lived near the Ocean, no matter where, all had roughly the same lifestyle as all other people living near the ocean. They could have lived thousands of miles from each other, yet their lives were similar. I have also noticed that mountain people tend to be more conservative in their isolation than seafarers are.

I originally set out to show how topography and climate could explain why we in the West are seemingly more adventurous and extraverted than the Asians. I soon realized that slicing up the planet into only two parts, East and West is an oversimplification. India does not fit into one camp or the other.

Many factors need to be taken into account. Another major influence that changed people's psyches was invasions by foreign armies. So, after I realized India's uniqueness, my two-tiered graph morphed into a three-tiered graph that perfectly mirrored an old chart of mine that represented our three energetic bodies. (See the graph on the next page.)

As you look inside the body at the bottom third, you will notice I refer to that area as energetically corresponding to Western civilization. That heading encompasses all the great civilizations that were originally influenced by the Egyptians, which includes the Greeks, Romans, Jews, and by extension, most of modern Europe and America. My first observation was that the Nile River area had some of the most ideal topography in the world for speeding up our evolution on all levels of life. It consistently supported a lush climate coupled with predictable seasonal flooding that laid down fresh deposits of mineral-rich silt every year. That scenario alone created a food surplus, which afforded the leisure time necessary to create a great civilization.

Nature accommodated the Nile River area in another way that made transportation up and down the river practically effortless.

+ PLUSES	MINUSES -	
India's genius goes to SPIRIT & MIND **Nature is an illusion** The Holy Person is most respected	INDIA IS INTO UNITY, ONENESS	SPIRITUALITY This is their strength SOCIALLY India's caste system is repressive MATERIALLY Poverty & filth Abound
China's genius goes to SOCIETY **Nature is to be intuited** The Scholar/Sage is most respected.	CHINA IS INTO SOCIETY, GROUP PSYCHOLOGY	SPIRITUALITY No interest in spiritual matters SOCIALLY This is their strength MATERIALLY Recent progress
The West's genius goes to the MATERIAL WORLD **Nature is to be conquered** The Wealthy Person is most respected	THE WEST IS INTO THE EXTERNAL WORLD, MATERIALISM	SPIRITUALITY Aggressive and intolerant SOCIALLY Fragmented MATERIALLY This is their strength

The Nile flows downstream into the Mediterranean, and the hot air over Africa pulls the winds upstream, so all the Egyptians had to do was put up their sails to be pushed effortlessly upstream. When the material world is this abundant and cooperative, it also allows the leisure time needed to create a written language that in turn makes it easier to proliferate information, passing this acquired knowledge from one generation to the next. Indeed, knowledge is power.

As the popular saying goes, there are three things necessary for commercial success: location, location, location. This was certainly another huge advantage for the Nile River region. When people are situated near many other peoples and bodies of water, this encourages the speedy dissemination of goods and ideas around the area. Being at the nexus of two continents sharing the same latitude and similar climate further accelerated trade and made it easier to share philosophies and inventions. Most ideas and inventions do not easily spread north and south on the continents due to extreme climatic and topographical barriers, and environments with different problems and needs require different solutions.

As you can see from the chart, the energy of the people in the West corresponds roughly to the lower part of the human body, which is mostly concerned with the gathering, transporting, and transforming the material world into useable energy. Our most significant contributions to humanity have resulted from our fascination with the material plane, which manifests as our emphasis on science, exploration, physical health, and the exploitation of the material world. We feel compelled to measure everything, and the person with the most material possessions is the most revered in our societies.

With so much emphasis on the material plane, it leaves us rather weak in the interpersonal, social realms (the middle, social center of the chart). We are not quite the melting pot of the world we are given credit for. Look at our social prejudices and divorce rate. Our "rule by conflict of interest" usually ends up with hundreds of splinter groups unable to reach consensus on much of anything these days. Even our religions cannot achieve unity. There are over 250 Protestant denominations, for Christ's sake!

While our social skills are weak, our transcendent, spiritual skills (represented by the upper spiritual level of the chart) are practically non-existent. Keep in mind I draw a sharp distinction between being spiritual and being religious because my definition of spirituality necessitates transcendence. Of course, you can be both, but there is a lot of churchgoing in this country and very little transcendence. Part of the problem is that our dominant religions put an emphasis on the material realm. We will resurrect bodily as Jesus did, and the kingdom of heaven will come to this Earth, etc. Any talk of discarnate, non-material, transcendent beings is still met with scorn and skepticism in this country.

Still, our social and spiritual shortcomings do not minimize our significant medical and other scientific contributions to humanity. Our staunch individualism, inquisitiveness, creativity, and high energy (nurtured by the environment around the Nile Valley) have contributed enormously to the overall physical wellbeing of most people on our planet. Better hygiene, better health care, more food, and more leisure-creating devices all contribute to our ever-rising life expectancy.

Now let's look into how topography created social genius in China. Imagine living in an area completely hemmed in on all sides by its topography and mostly isolated from the rest of humanity for thousands of years. That would be China, and you would end up with a society similar to the one that emerged in that area. The Han people of ancient China had endless wastelands to the north, oceans to the east and south, and vast deserts with the Himalayas and Kun Lun Mountains to the west.

With very little land available for farming, and everyone squeezed into that isolated bowl, they had two choices: kill everyone else or learn how to get along. After trying the former, they eventually chose the latter. Aided by the social genius of Confucius and the unification of the warring states under the ruthless Chin emperor, they managed to unify themselves at a fairly early stage in human evolution. This offered a big advantage over other civilizations that didn't unify so soon and had no enduring written language.

Having a written language more than 3,000 years old and – unlike the Egyptian language – characters with a built-in flexibility to evolve more complex characters, the Chinese eventually forged one of the planet's most enduring societies.

And don't forget how innovative the Chinese were – and still are – with the material world. They invented gunpowder, the printing press (some 400 years before Gutenberg!), and the compass – all of which changed the destiny of the whole world. They also have no Neanderthal genes in their DNA, so of course, they are smarter than we Westerners. Now on to India....

At the upper part of the chart is the spiritual level and the many spiritual contributions of India, or the nation of Bharat, as they call themselves. That vast country has given birth to some of the world's greatest religions: Hinduism, Buddhism, and Jainism. All three focus primarily on transcendence – and in complete contrast to China, they have incredibly rich mythologies.

Actually, Hinduism is not a single religion. It is a collection of religions and cultural traditions. The main religious groups we call Hindus today include Vaishnavites, Shaivites, Sikhs, Tantrikas, and Shaktas. In India, unlike China and the West, holy people are the most highly respected. Enlightenment for most of them means transcending the world of rebirth and duality and merging with the great Oneness. Most regard the material world as illusion, and if you look at a topographical map of India, you will quickly understand why.

The upper part of that country is an inhospitable mountain range (the Himalayas). Below that is the Thar Desert, which covers thousands of square miles. Below that, it is hot as hell, with debilitating monsoon rains every year. All you want to do is lie in a hammock and drink beer for most of the year.

In spite of all that, and similarly to China, India has produced some of the greatest minds and most highly evolved spiritual people on the planet, in my opinion. It seems like India gives birth to a spiritual giant every hundred years or so, and their visionary pundits were exploring concepts of the unconscious long before Freud developed and popularized it.

There's no doubt people are different in the ways they think and live, and now I have no doubt that topography is strongly instrumental in shaping their psyches in significant ways.

So, get outside and take advantage of the power of Nature to heal you both physically and psychologically. Researchers have just found that people who spend a few minutes walking around in nature or fussing in a garden every day live longer and are more content than those who sit at a desk all day.

And be sure to walk barefoot when possible because my teacher constantly said that our feet are capable of absorbing the energy of the Earth through acupuncture point kidney #1 on the soles of our feet. Unfortunately, the only energy the soles of our feet are exposed to these days is rubber and leather! When I walk barefoot, I often feel my feet tingling, then turning red. It is very energizing also!

But enough about Feng Shui and topology. I regularly taught several other workshops that had enormous influences on everyone's health. Now onto the Chinese nine chakras/vortices and how to heal yourself with them.

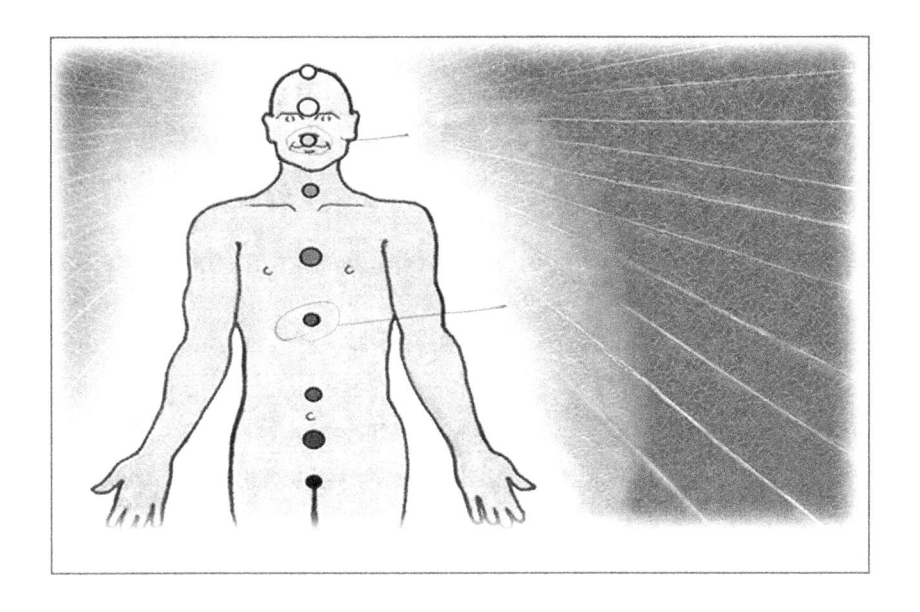

THE NINE DAOIST VORTICES

Not too many people even know about this particular Chinese system, but most of those who do, say it has transformed their lives. It is similar to the Hindu chakra system, only the Daoists recognize nine chakras instead of seven, and they call them vortices. Most people know how to keep their physical bodies healthy (although they too often don't do it). Some know how to stimulate their meridian system with acupressure/acupuncture treatments and Chi Gung exercises. However, very few know how to keep their vortices stimulated and integrated.

This chapter will show you how to do it. It is one of the most advanced techniques I taught in my workshops. The chart on the next page integrates several versions my teachers taught me over the years. Unlike acupuncture points, the nine vortices are not specific spots. They are small fields of energy rotating and vibrating at a certain frequency. There are three groups of three – lower, middle, and upper. The middle vortex ("sacral") relates to sexuality and creativity. This energy stimulates us to pump out babies faster than the tigers can eat them!

The lowest three vortices are our connection to the Earth and are called pre-personal because they can exist before a personality has evolved. They are capable of operating without any conscious awareness. (It certainly seemed like my sexual energy operated for over 50 years without much conscious intervention.)

The lowest of these three vortices is located at the perineum. The next one up is just below the navel and is the largest vortex of the group. The uppermost vortex in the group is just above the navel. Many of my spiritual friends tend to ignore these three. They think they are being more spiritual by focusing only on the highest group.

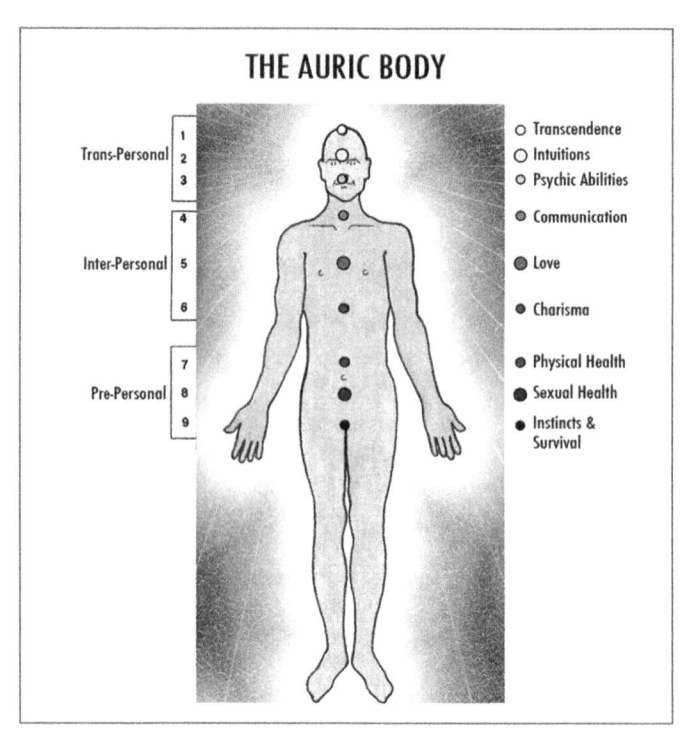

THE AURIC BODY

Trans-Personal	1	○ Transcendence
	2	○ Intuitions
	3	○ Psychic Abilities
Inter-Personal	4	◐ Communication
	5	◐ Love
	6	● Charisma
Pre-Personal	7	● Physical Health
	8	● Sexual Health
	9	● Instincts & Survival

They do this to their peril. The three lowest vortices are critical to our survival. To ignore the bottom one, in particular, renders people vulnerable to accidents. I had a student who only meditated on his uppermost vortex to speed up liberation from his body. It worked. He stepped in front of a rapidly moving car one afternoon. If he had detoxed and stimulated the lowest one along with all the others, his instincts would have automatically responded to the approaching vehicle, and he might still be alive today. Stimulation of that vortex has saved me many times. (I provide details later in the chapter titled Playing with Death and Immortality.) The lowest vortex, called the "root" in modern terminology, relates to our instincts and survival. For example, if a tiger is attacking you, the energy of the lowest vortex stimulates you to run like hell – or at least to run faster than the slowest person in your group!

The upper one, which happens to be one of the two vortices unique to the Daoist system and located just above the navel, is where our physical body is governed for obvious reasons - it is where our physical body grew from. This energy strengthens the notion that if we're not physically healthy, we can't make babies or run fast enough to escape the tigers – or vehicles, as the case may be.

Moving up the body, we reach the middle three vortices, which are our connection to other people, and it is called "interpersonal." The lowest of the three in the middle group is located at the solar plexus, the larger middle one is located at the heart center, and the upper one is in the center of the throat. The vortex at the bottom houses the energy of charisma and animal magnetism. Many politicians are highly developed in this area, and it is this vortex I suggest my women students develop in order to be heard and felt in social situations. The middle and largest vortex of this group is the "heart" vortex. This is the center of love and compassion. I have observed that if you don't love yourself, you cannot truly love anyone else, so be sure to include this aspect of the process first.

An example of not loving yourself enough would be if you overlook caring for your own physical, emotional/mental, and spiritual health. Consider…do you take better care of your dog and your car than you care for yourself?

The heart vortex is the one we all need to develop more.

The "throat" vortex, located at the top of the middle group, is the one I tell my male students to work on because we males are usually pathetic at communicating feelings. Effective communication is often more difficult for us than having the feeling in the first place. My female friends have often asked me if I have ever had a feeling. I constantly assure them that, of course, I do – I feel hungry every day.

Continuing upward, the three upper vortices, all located in the head, are called transpersonal because they are often beyond the control of our personality. The lowest of the three is at the base of the nose. The middle one is slightly above and between the eyebrows. The upper one is on the top of the head.

The bottom vortex of this group (the second vortex exclusive to the Daoist system is located under the nose) is good for developing psychic abilities and alleviating epileptic seizures. Many acupuncturists use this point for epilepsy, and sometimes you can do it yourself. Pressing on it with your middle finger and sending chi inward and upward to the part of the brain that causes seizures will often stop them. If not, then find a good acupuncturist or Qi Gong instructor.

The center and largest vortex, located between and slightly above the eyebrows, stimulates our intuitive abilities. It also stimulates the pituitary gland, which is considered the body's master gland. This vortex is often referred to as the "third eye." The uppermost of all the vortices ("crown") allows transcendence to occur more easily. If it is stimulated regularly enough, the energy going through it makes the top of the skull in that area soft. That is why Daoists refer to it as "the mud pill." Its becoming soft encourages out-of-body and transcendent experiences.

Whenever we Daoists work with any vortex of the body, we always visualize stabilizing its frequency first. Then we stimulate it.

You begin this process by using the middle finger on your right hand to stabilize each vortex. Start from the top and work your way down. Tap each vortex nine times while repeating the related phrase. Put the emphasis on your exhale while stabilizing in a downward direction. Repeat the following phrases nine times while touching the appropriate descending energy center:

Crown
"That which obstructs transcendence descends into the Earth."

Third Eye
"That which obstructs my intuition descends into the Earth."

Under Nose
"That which obstructs my psychic abilities
descends into the Earth."

Throat
"That which obstructs my ability to communicate love and wisdom descends into the Earth."

Heart
"That which obstructs my love of myself and others
descends into the Earth."

Solar Plexus
"That which obstructs my influence in the world (charisma)
descends into the Earth."

Above the Navel
"That which obstructs my physical health descends into the Earth."

Sacral
"That which obstructs my sexual and creative health descends into the Earth."

Root
"That which obstructs my instincts and survival descends into the Earth."

After stabilizing all nine centers from top to bottom, use the middle finger of your left hand to stimulate and enhance each of the nine vortices from the bottom up. While working your way up the nine vortices, the emphasis is now on the inhalation, so hold your breath while stimulating. Repeat the phrases nine times at each vortex, as shown in the following ascending direction.

Root
"That which enhances my instincts and survival I attract to this vortex."

Sacral
"That which enhances my sexual and creative health I attract to this vortex."

Above the Navel
"That which enhances my physical health I attract to this vortex."

Solar Plexus
"That which enhances my influence in the world (charisma) I attract to this vortex."

Heart
"That which enhances my love of myself and others
I attract to this vortex."

Throat
"That which enhances my ability to communicate love
and wisdom I attract to this vortex."

Under the Nose
"That which enhances my psychic abilities
I attract to this vortex."

Third Eye
"That which enhances my intuition
I attract to this vortex."

Crown
"That which enhances transcendence
I attract to this vortex."

After completing this two-part process, spend a few quiet minutes being aware of your three bodies at the same time: the physical, bioelectric, and auric. Feel your heart beating, your lungs moving, and the pressure on your feet. Then experience yourself as a mass of bioelectricity flowing through your meridians. Then spend a few minutes experiencing yourself as pure white light extending out to the ends of the Universe. You might find the individual colors of your vortices merging into white as they expand out into the infinite vastness. While doing this quietly standing, be open and allow their integration. Release all thinking, feeling, and intentions. Developing the capacity to be completely open generally takes about 40 years – so get started. After ten minutes of "empty standing and allowing," many students leave class in a state of euphoria.

> *Being open and allowing the high-frequency energy to flow through your three bodies is what Play is all about!*

However, integration of the three bodies is only the beginning. As you cultivate and integrate your more subtle aspects, you start to recognize your personal spirit is identical to the over-soul, or the Oneness. You realize you are more than a physical body with a spirit. You can experience all life as spirit, which includes the other two bodies and the rest of the Universe. Eventually, you identify less and less with anything personal, and you begin to truly love your neighbor as yourself because he is yourself! Until then, that sentence is just a slogan. Identifying with only one of your three bodies becomes a problem when a person knows nothing other than the one body. It eventually feels very constrictive because the spirit knows it is not all there is to Self. It is like being in jail. But when the doors of this larger perception are open, and you are free to come or go, any one of your bodies becomes more like a fake jail in a fun house – just another Playground for the Playful! Your identifying with only one body is simply a case of mistaken identity.

> *To the extent you identify with anything less than everything, you are mistaken as to who you truly are.*

When the awareness of identifying with everything becomes an abiding state instead of a temporary realization, some individuals leave the body and cease to reincarnate, while others stay for the sake of helping humanity. When you realize you ARE the great Oneness, the boundary lines, and therefore the battle lines between you and everything else dissolves…and there is peace.

Here are a two quick visualizations to remind you of the underlying oneness of everything.

Imagine you are a whirlpool of water in the ocean. Water molecules swirl into and down around your particular shape and then leave from the bottom of the whirlpool you identify with. They then flow out into the vastness of the ocean. If a whirlpool is simply the ocean temporarily swirling around a particular shape, why identify with one whirlpool to the exclusion of all other whirlpools and the rest of the ocean? Finally, consider your dreams. Everything in your dreams is your own projection. The background on which all the dream images appear is also your creation, as is the dreamer and all the characters in your dreams – be aware you are the totality of everything you are dreaming!

So, be aware you are the totality of everything you are dreaming. These perspectives were most eloquently expressed by Yogic philosopher Ramesh S. Balsekar:

Consciousness has written the script.

Consciousness has produced this play.

Consciousness is playing all the characters.

And consciousness is witnessing the play.

It's a one-being show!

TEACHING DAOIST SEXUAL CULTIVATION

I saved my most interesting teaching experience for last. No workshops drew bigger crowds than the ones I taught on Daoist sexuality (also known as dual cultivation.) The particular technique I will be going into is the one most people actually got the greatest benefit from.

In those days, many young Americans had just survived the 20-year era of "free love" and were wondering whether all that free love was worth the price. For many, sex had become little more than two anxious bodies banging together in a frantic attempt to eke out a little pleasure in their otherwise meaningless lives of chronic stress and depression. The idea of sex as a possible conduit to their experiencing oneness with the other brought new meaning and greater dimensions into their lives, something people very much needed at the time.

This may surprise you, but after a few months of practice, many people reported having profound spiritual experiences while making love. It didn't matter whether it was within marriage or not, or whether it was with the opposite or same sex. As long as love was involved and a willingness to be open to deeper energetic experiences, it seemed to happen spontaneously.

Daoist sexual energy cultivations are not to be confused with the more popular Hindu Tantric practices, even though they originally had much in common. They both started out as an embodied participation in cosmic principles. However, they both eventually degenerated into little more than "screwing for God," or as the Buddhists called it, "screwing for the benefit of all mankind." The main difference: Chinese dual cultivation is mostly bioelectrical in emphasis and involves the chi flowing through the meridians of the two bodies. More common practices involve having sex in different positions to cure different diseases, while the higher ones involve the auric bodies and are beyond the scope of this book. Since there are plenty of books on Daoist sexuality these days, here is the one I taught the most.

A man's fiery yang energies tend to rise, causing broad shoulders, baldness, and aggressive tendencies. A women's watery yin energy tends to sink, aiding menstrual flow, causing broad hips and emotional extremes. Thus, they are instructed to sit in the lotus position with the man below the woman. She sits on his lap with her legs wrapped around his waist. That way, his rising energy interpenetrates her sinking energy in a very natural and powerful way. The position of yang energy being under the yin energy is also regarded as being highly auspicious and more unifying by certain hexagrams (energetic arrangements) found in the Chinese classic, the *Book of Changes*.

After getting physically plugged in, the couple is encouraged to coordinate their breathing, so they are alternately inhaling and exhaling. They then coordinate their minds to focus on the same spot on one of their bodies. For instance, they both focus on the lower spine of the woman and coordinate their breathing as he exhales, and she inhales the combined energy (chi) up her spine and over her head. Then she exhales, and he inhales it down the front of her body into his penis. Their combined chi flow and coordinated breathing then circulates up his spine and over his head and down the front of his body into his penis. From there, it travels to the base of her spine, and the circulation continues. The energy circulating around the two bodies resembles an infinity sign in the shape of water wings.

Around and around their bodies the combined chi flows, gathering strength as it circulates. After a while, both people cease the guided flow and just relax to let it happen on its own. A few times, I have had the experience of the chi circulating faster and faster until it rises out the top of both of our heads like a double helix and merges into a combined total body ecstasy for both people. If that experience does not happen on the first attempt, try, try again is my motto. Don't misunderstand me; an orgasm limited to the genitals is not that horrible, but I must admit, I feel sorry for people who only experience genital sex.

In addition to dual cultivation, my Chinese teacher also taught us how to give birth to a highly evolved child, and my daughter is living testimony to the success of those instructions. Too many people have sex at the wrong time, in the worst of circumstances, and for all the wrong reasons. They then wonder why they have given birth to a difficult child. If you make love during a hurricane while drunk and angry with your spouse, what kind of soul is going to be attracted to that energetic circumstance?

Contrary to those who think we consciously choose our parents – we don't. Our soul gravitates to like frequencies of energy that it resonates with – which is more an energy response than a conscious decision. This is similar to how most of us make friends in the physical world. According to my teacher, we mostly gravitate toward certain people rather than it being a conscious decision.

My teacher also observed that we are willing to spend an inordinate amount of time and money trying to rehabilitate all the damaged souls we have brought into this world. Yet hardly anyone is willing to devote a few months to spiritually prepare themselves for the blessed event of birthing a new soul.

No matter how much love and devotion you give to your little "Attila the Hun," he or she is going to be trouble for a long time. Of course, perfect parenting will soften the impact of the troubled child you just gave birth to, but why not attract a highly-evolved being into the world as long as you are busily creating babies? I have heard that children do not come into the world with a clean slate and that research is now discovering the agenda babies bring with them. We parents are here to love and guide them on their already established karmic pathways, and that is about the best we can do. I have observed that highly-evolved children are low maintenance, and it is a pure joy to watch their further evolution.

In addition, if you want a highly-evolved person to stay around after conception, follow these tips to create the most positive energy field for the growth of the baby in the womb. The prospective parents should do Chi Gung daily or whatever helps detox their bodies and minds. Anything that stimulates cellular communication and lymphatic flow is good for detoxification. They should eat a healthy diet for those nine months, and you know what that means: no junk food, alcohol, or stimulants of any kind. They should meditate more than usual and be pure in their thoughts and actions while allowing for the high being to have a healthy birth and life. And don't forget, ordinary genital orgasm by the male is necessary to start the process – despite how disgustingly limited it is. If you are really serious about attracting a highly evolved being, there are other energy cultivations you can do and auspicious energy days on which to conceive. There are also herbal pouches a woman can wear, and there are certain Feng Shui arrangements you can make to enhance your chances of attracting a more evolved spirit.

Any good acupuncturist can help you with those issues, but I want you to take the whole process of bringing more children into this turbulent world more seriously. So in the following chapter, I have assembled all you need to know about making good decisions in your life.

Playing While Thinking

After all that "spiritual doing," it was time in my life to do some "spiritual thinking." It was the 1980s, and I was still teaching a number of classes and workshops around the country. I was learning a lot from my students, as my teacher predicted, but no one taught me more than Ken Wilber in those days. His theories changed my life, and I have been teaching his perspectives with my practices ever since.

Before sharing a few of his ideas, I would like to clarify some erroneous spiritual thinking about spiritual thinking. A few religions, the Zen Buddhists, for example, insist that an overly busy mind is an impediment to enlightenment – tell that to Leonardo Da Vinci! I do agree our minds must be trained, but some gurus I have known have gone so far as to say that enlightenment or oneness with everything is only possible when the mind is perfectly still, which is only partially true.

Have you considered how many truly inspired and creative thoughts and insights come to us each day as part of our intuitive processes? If you insist on always staying mentally focused on the "here and now," you might miss out on a lot of inspiration in your life. It is important to make sure your thoughts don't run your life. I spent several years focused on every bite of food I was eating and constantly scanning my body for messages. I can only imagine how many subtle, intuitive impulses I must have missed at that time because of that narrow focus.

> *You are the great Oneness*
> *whether you believe it or not,*
> *or whether you are thinking or not.*

Many people are like frogs down in their wells. They shout out, "Come on down and check out this nourishing water we have here. Have you ever seen a more impressive body of water in your life?" As a toad from the lake who has visited many wells, I just shout back, "I have no doubt your water is nourishing but come on out and get a bigger picture, then return to your well if you still want to."

Having a larger picture opens the door to more possibilities in life. It allows you to move freely between your transcendent self, your mental self, your psychological self, and your physical self. In other words, you have access to more levels of your being.

This is not as difficult as it sounds. It is very much like the many ways you can experience yourself as the Ocean.

One minute you could identify with a particular wave rolling merrily along, minding its own business. The next thing, you might be a vast, calm Sea. If you prefer, you can even experience the powerful undercurrents that lie below the surface.

If the Ocean and the Universe have all these levels of expression, then you do also because you are a miniature version of the Universe and more. All possibilities exist, so don't cut yourself off from any of the myriad ways to Play and enjoy your life, regardless of what aspect you are identifying with at the moment.

I suspect you are currently identifying with someone going by your name on Planet Earth, so wouldn't it be fun to know where we as individuals and we as a species came from, the stage we are in now, and what we might expect in our future evolution?

Does the phrase "ontogeny recapitulates phylogeny" ring a bell? If not, it simply means that the unfolding process of every individual is mirrored by the unfolding stages of human evolution. That means that each person – regardless of nationality, race, or gender – goes through the same stages of growth and in the same order. There are still groups of people alive today who represent the most primitive stages of development and mindset, so it's important to remember that everyone's perspective is correct and true for them, no matter what stage they are in. It might take many more lifetimes, but eventually, everyone will come to know their innate Oneness with everything that is and is not.

Everyone's perspective is partial, and everyone's potential is the same.

I once heard a talk that clearly illustrated the true and partial view of the different mindsets. It went something like this:

An illiterate person living in a small village in the remote jungles of South America stumbles upon a book on quantum physics. He examines it carefully and very cleverly decided it would be great for starting fires. He was right.

Then a young modern child finds it and knows it is a book but can't read it, so she keeps it as a precious possession that has magical powers in it. She enjoyed every minute she had it.

Her father, an explorer, reads the book but throws it away because it made no sense to him. He was justified in his reaction because quantum mechanics seems nonsensical to those not familiar with the subject.

Then a quantum physicist finds it and is incredibly inspired by it. He is so impressed that he shows it to his guru/sage friend who appreciates the new insights but also laments the limited ability of words to clearly describe the basic nature of reality.

Everyone's perception of the book is correct and also partial. AND they are all impoverished views of reality – including mine. The following is my version of the major milestones every individual and society goes through in the slow, upward evolutionary spiral of humanity. My simple understanding was inspired by the works of Ken Wilber, Jean Gebser, Jean Piaget, Don Beck, Christopher Cowan, and many others. One of the more exciting discoveries of the last 50 years is that the human race is going through the same stages an individual does, only at a much slower rate.

Having a better idea as to how and where life is evolving clears up a lot of confusion and aids in our ability to communicate with the different mindsets. There is nothing more challenging and in more desperate need of improvement these days than communicating more effectively with one another. Here are the stages everyone and all societies go through.

INFANCY – Individual
Everyone (except avatars) comes into life at the instinctual, survival level. There are only biological needs at this stage, and there is no awareness of self as a distinct entity. Every newborn is immersed in the subconscious realms of nature, and there is no sense of time.

INFANCY – Society
Starting about five million years ago to roughly 50,000 years ago, the hunter-gatherers represented the social equivalent of this stage of personal development. Small groups of people lived off the land, living timelessly in the present, pretty much the same as other animals.

EARLY CHILDHOOD – Individual

This is the time in everyone's life when our sense of self as separate from everything else begins to form, although we are still largely undifferentiated. The newly emergent ego lives in a scary and magical world. Safety needs are paramount, and allegiance is limited to parents and family.

EARLY CHILDHOOD – Society

At this stage of social evolution, 50,000 to around 12,000 years ago (the advent of agriculture), people lived in small and large tribes. Many groups were matriarchal, and everyone lived in an animated world in which spirits were everywhere. This era was characterized by taboos, totems, hexes, omens, sacrifices (human and animal), and during this period, shamanism emerged. In this pre-literate phase, continuity was sustained through stories, music, and dance.

LATE CHILDHOOD – Individual

As the ego develops, the child begins to experience the parents as being all-powerful. From age three to twelve, order is restored after the parents survive the brief era of the "terrible twos" – unless the two-year-old takes control over the entire family!

LATE CHILDHOOD – Society

In the mostly patriarchal societies after 5,000 BC until around 1,000 AD, when personal, egoic magic was exposed as having little substance behind it, and the spells no longer had the same effect, the mythical gods Amun-Ra, Zeus, Jupiter, Yahweh, and Thor became the unquestioned parental figures of their era. This gave new order and meaning to people's lives, and the written word became the glue that held the empires and religions together.

ADOLESCENCE – Individual

Autonomy and independent thought rears its pimple-faced head, and rebellion against authority ensues with the onset of adolescence.

This awkward phase that marks the advent of personal power often comes without the emotional maturity to control it. The rational mind starts to differentiate between things and seeks evidence and understanding, but the more basic impulses are still strong at this stage of personal development.

ADOLESCENCE – Society

The scientific revolution is the social equivalent of adolescence in an individual. It started around 1500 AD and continues to the present. Evolution itself seems to speed up in this phase. The scientific, industrial, entrepreneurial era is upon us with a vengeance – starkly and sadly characterized by hydrogen bombs in the hands of the spiritually immature. The pragmatic, scientific perspective starts to topple the mythical gods, and religious uncertainty ensues. Consumerism is the new god, and the CEOs of transnational corporations are the new global masters. You probably recognize that adolescence is the evolutionary level humanity finds itself in now. May we survive it!

ADULTHOOD – Individual

This is the time when we learn cooperation, with unity and vision being supported by logic and a synthesizing mode of cognition. Ignoring or eliminating differences – as we might have tried in our earlier stages of life – no longer works. At this stage, people are forced to embrace differences, and many attempt to find unity in diversity. Each person is valued, and the individual's perspective has evolved from national egocentric to global ecocentric.

ADULTHOOD – Society

Because most societies are not yet at this stage of development, this process of social evolution still lies in the future of humankind. Provided we do not blow ourselves up in the meantime, the gravitational mass of humanity will surely catch up with the visionary trailblazers who are busily applying themselves to right the wrongs of individual and corporate greed, freeing us from the immature applications of technologies that are wreaking havoc on our biosphere.

MATURE ADULTHOOD – Individual
This is the spiritual/integrative time of life. The kids are grown, and there is time to ponder the meaning of life, time to further one's spiritual growth, and give back to society.

MATURE ADULTHOOD – Society
This is the first level in which one is capable of appreciating all the other perspectives. Only at the mature adult stage do people respect (but not necessarily agree with) all the other worldviews and are able to appreciate "both/and" solutions to challenges rather than fall back to "either/or" positions. Also, notice that prior to this new stage, each stage looked down at the previous stage with contempt and viewed the level above it with suspicion, if not outright fear. For example, when the mythic religions reigned supreme, they mostly had contempt for the tribes they unified under their god. In time, they came to fear the rational and secular views of the scientific materialism paradigm.

In the same way, at the next level, most scientists, engineers, and entrepreneurs had nothing but scorn for the mythic religions, while they resist the emerging influence of the idealistic green movement because they regard those tree-hugging environmentalists as an impediment to progress.

Further up the evolutionary spiral are the idealistic and global visionary people, who are dedicated to a green and peaceful environment yet despise the nasty scientific/entrepreneurial perspective they grew out of. They also view the emerging staunch individualism of the mature adult level as threatening to their communal, mostly inept, politically correct herd mentality.

Einstein famously said that you couldn't solve a problem using the same level of thinking that created it. In other words, you cannot solve complex national disputes with a tribal mentality. You cannot solve global problems with an "only my God is right" religious perspective, and, likewise, we will never solve intergalactic squabbles with only a global perspective. Evolution is a process, and individuals and societies find themselves at different stages of that process. None of these stages are "right" or "wrong." Rather than trying to change people, we are better off approaching them at whatever level they are at. This perspective holds that all worldviews are legitimate, and there are healthy and balanced people at all levels. Our present task is to facilitate communication between the various perspectives and deepen our connection with one another. This will lead to greater harmony among people and a more complete view of life that is seen from varied perspectives.

Many of our social and religious misunderstandings have been caused by the interaction of people at different stages of development. Even within a particular religion, you can have followers at many different levels of awareness and sophistication. The best hope for eventual integration of all perspectives will come from this broad perspective and the later stages of evolution.

WIZARD/AVATAR – Individual

Very few individuals have evolved to this stage of evolution, so there is not much understanding about what they are like, and it will be a long time before the masses of humanity get there. This book is one attempt to describe people I have known who are at this level. There is a love, awareness, mystery, and power about those people that perfectly reflects the deep power and mystery of the cosmos. It seems they have an intuitive ability to see everything at once, which gives them a broad range of behavioral options. Their conscious and subconscious minds work together, so they do not just "go with the flow," they somehow co-create the flow. They Play with paradox and chaos. The ability to transform and bring out the best in everyone with whom they come into contact is one of the surest signs you are in the presence of a wizard/avatar. I cannot wait until the majority of the human race has evolved to the level of a Buddha, a Lao Tzu, a Jesus, or a Ramana Maharshi – and beyond!

WIZARD/AVATAR – Society

Another interesting trend to notice with these various perspectives is that humanity spirals from a group mentality to the power of the individual and back to the group again. This applies to all levels of the spiral. For example, people like Alexander the Great, Julius Caesar, and Genghis Khan united the city-states wherever they went. Then the religious group mentality brought order and meaning to the decimated world the conquerors created. Out of the religious herd mentality came individual scientists who shook the foundations of the religions. Out of the divisive scientific and corporate CEO mentality (the Genghis Khans of the present era) came the need for a global community that emphasizes consensus and harmony. Out of the inefficient and stifling collectivism of the "politically correct crowd" came strong, mature individuals who emphasize getting things done while still retaining a global mentality. With that swing of the pendulum to the individual, the next stage of evolution will be when all the strong individuals learn how to get along together (no easy task). I have heard it said that the next coming of the Christ would not be an individual but a group of people sharing the same consciousness.

Out of that rarefied atmosphere of shared consciousness will come the individual sage/wizards: trans-humans who will embody a fluidity, spontaneity, magic, and mystery the likes of which the world has not yet seen. This trajectory of evolution will continue right up to intergalactic subtle beings that are as close to the "Source" as you can get in a manifest world. And we won't be limited to this planet.

Another aspect of all this is to remember that evolution happens exponentially. This means you can only predict the future in very general terms because the curve of innovation and complexity rises rapidly, which creates more chaos and unpredictability.

Some predict the age of the avatars will happen in 35 years. That is a bit too optimistic for me, but the trans-humanists predict there is nothing stopping us from doing our own conscious evolution right now. Soon, there will be no need to wait for Mother Nature to continue our biological evolution. We can take the reins ourselves with the genome and DNA breakthroughs, nanotechnology, cloning, neuroscience, neuropharmacology, artificial intelligence, life extension, biological immortality, chimera creation, and space habitation. Of course, we must be sure to temper artificial intelligence with REAL intelligence.

By enhancing our bodies, minds, and environments, a whole new order of what it means to be human will arise. In an age where robots will have biological parts, sophisticated emotions, and self-awareness, and where we biological humans will have computer parts that increase our intelligence tenfold, with artificial organs and limbs, it will be ever more difficult to define what it truly means to be human. And these are all predicted to occur in the not too distant future. So stick around. It is going to get interesting!

Admitting all that is possible, I am concerned about whether it can all be done wisely, considering our present, rather adolescent state of being. An example of our current level of immaturity are the present-day neuroscientists who claim our consciousness, emotions, thoughts, habits, and even spiritual experiences are a product of synapses firing in our brains. They assert that if there is no brain, there is no awareness of any kind. They remind me of children playing with the inside of a TV set. They squeal with delight as they push buttons and cross wires and are able to influence the picture and sound. "See," they say, "this is proof that our brains create the picture and sound because we have complete control over everything that happens." I keep hoping they soon discover the brain is only receiving high-frequency signals from the great oneness, sometimes trillions of miles away, just like the TV is receiving signals from a distant TV station! Alas, so much knowledge, so little wisdom!

Certain religious perspectives are just as immature as the scientists. I recently saw a program that showed a conservative Christian museum that was displaying dinosaurs in the animal lineup going into the ark! (More on the flood story later.) Their literal interpretation of the Bible tells them that the Earth is only 6,000 years old, so instead of admitting they are wrong, they squeeze the scientific archeological discoveries into their mythical stories! Any religion that continues to cling to its myths as fact and does not allow for evolution or any other challenge to its stories will not survive the next 25 years.

At any rate, relax and enjoy all the future discoveries and changes that are bound to happen soon. We Integralists use one more important tool that can be inserted horizontally into Beck and Cowan's evolutionary spiral. It is Wilber's four-quadrant grid that can bring clarity to any moment or situation we find ourselves in. Once you understand and use it, you can begin to eliminate a lot of unnecessary pain and suffering in your life.

Interior Subjective The inner "I" realm	**Exterior tangible subjective** The outer "It" realm
Interior Collective The inner "We" realm	**Exterior tangible collective** The outer "Its" realm

The idea of the quadrants is that every situation has four major aspects to it (some systems have eight, but four is enough to get started). If any of the four facets are ignored, there will be trouble, or at least your perspective or undertaking will be partial. The quadrants can be understood better in the following example.

Suppose you decide to move to a warmer city to escape the cold. Most people simply look at houses in the new area and move into the first nice home they find. However, that's when all hell can break loose. If you do not do the upper left quadrant work, you might move into a perfectly good home in a nice area and regret it for the rest of your life because you didn't closely examine why you really wanted to move in the first place. If loneliness or fear was the real reason you decided to move, then chances are those motivations will keep you discontented in the new place. The interior subjective (upper left) aspect of many people's lives is often not examined or clearly understood, and the result is pain in one form or another.

Suppose your inner motives for moving were honestly examined, but you didn't pay enough attention to the house you chose. That is the exterior, tangible subjective place (upper right quadrant) where your interior, subjective self will live. As a result of not checking out that quadrant, you discover termites after you move in, and the place has to be torn down – more pain.

Suppose your inner motives and the exterior house are great, but you don't look carefully into the collective interior (lower left quadrant) of the area in which you now live. The significance of your being the first black person to live in that area went unnoticed until you discovered all your neighbors belong to the Ku Klux Klan! There could be plenty of pain for that little oversight.

Suppose all of the above is fine but, after you move in, you discover the area is in a place called "tornado alley," or your property is situated over an old toxic waste dump, or the area is economically depressed. In other words, the collective tangible exterior (lower right quadrant) of the area was ignored, and you end up dead or on disability for the rest of your life because your body is poisoned. As you can see, it is vitally important that all four quadrants are addressed with every big decision in life, or the results could be disastrous.

I am sure you get the idea by now that if all four of those perspectives are not considered with every undertaking, progress will be slow and that undertaking might even end up at the undertaker's.

In summation, I hope you all clearly see the stages of maturity we all share and how the 4 Quadrants can help us make better decisions along the way. So NOW is the time to Grow Up – Wake Up – and Show Up in your life! Instead of searching for enlightenment all the time, look into your motives for seeking it! You cannot attain the here and now any more than you can "attain" your head. It's sitting right on your shoulders, just where you left it! So, relax and Play while allowing the Here and Now to flow through you…and now onto Playing with Famous People.

Playing with Famous People

Meanwhile, back in reality, in early 1982, I experienced another spectacular synchronicity.

It all started on a dark and stormy day in Los Angeles when I got a phone call from a friend who wanted me to go with him to a middle school summer camp on Mt. Palomar for the weekend. The camp was for young San Diego students who wanted some exposure to nature. They obviously needed it because I was amazed to see a cow in the pasture with the word "cow" painted on it. Since I was an amateur astronomer in those days, I was also excited at the prospect of seeing one of the world's largest telescopes during our free time.

The minute I arrived, I was shown a small Questar telescope that had been donated to the camp. The instructors at the camp said they could not figure out how to use it. Without any instruction booklet,

I struggled with it for the first two nights during my stay. On the third day, I was able to meet with the instructors and show them how to use it. That little telescope turned out to be an important talisman in another soon-to-be, life-altering encounter.

By the way, I was able to see the famous telescope on Mt. Palomar up close. It rained the day I arrived, and since I was the only visitor, they let me into the building after much pleading and begging on my part. I watched them do infra-red work, which is not affected by the weather. They were looking at the evolution of galaxies and exotic phenomena in active galactic nuclei. I even got to ride around in the cage that is attached to the back of the telescope.

When I returned home, there was a phone message saying Francis Ford Coppola wanted a Tai Chi teacher and that I should go in for an interview. The next day, the producer asked if I could be in Tulsa, Oklahoma in three days. I wasn't even sure where Oklahoma was, but off I went with my personal telescope sticking out of the sunroof of my car.

Upon arrival at the primary school the movie company rented for the summer, I was immediately taken to the gymnasium to meet Coppola and the cast and crew of *The Outsiders*. I had no idea what to say to break the ice because I considered actors to be overly-paid imitators and thought most movies were trash. In other words, I didn't have much in common with them.

As fate would have it, I didn't have to say anything. Coppola immediately asked if I had a place to stay. "I just arrived," I replied and pointed out the window of the gymnasium to my car in the parking lot. He saw my scope sticking out of the car and asked if it was a telescope. I said yes. He replied, "Carl Sagan recently gave me a small telescope, and I can't figure out how to use it." By some extraordinary coincidence (i.e., synchronicity) it was the same model scope I'd learned a few days before at summer camp.

The next thing I knew, we were both on our hands and knees in a corner of the gym discussing its use. Because of our mutual love of astronomy, one of my nightly duties, in addition to teaching everyone Tai Ji, was to set up the telescopes so the cast and crew could look at the stars between takes.

As I reflect upon the making of that movie and the following movie, *Rumble Fish*, which was shot back-to-back with *The Outsiders* in the same city, I now regard those times as magical – and not only in my life. It must have been a magical time for the whole film industry. Probably never before have two movies featured so many young and mostly unknown actors and actresses who later turned out to be megastars.

During those extraordinary times, I got to know the young Nicolas Cage, Tom Cruise, Diane Lane, Patrick Swayze, Matt Dillon, Rob Lowe, Laurence Fishburne, Ralph Macchio, Mickey Rourke, C. Thomas Howell, Emilio Estevez, and Tom Waits, along with others who visited us at the various locations. They

During the filming of The Outsiders, *Mark, on the left, taught Tai Ji to Francis Ford Coppola, Emilio Esteves, Rob Lowe, Tom Cruise, and C. Thomas Howell.*

were exceptionally talented youngsters running around having a good time. No big egos, no one was famous, and I enjoyed them all.

Although I liked them, I soon discovered that those people were more interested in making movies than in the precious gift I was giving them, so I soon became disenchanted with the whole scene. If it were not for Coppola's wife, Eleanor, and her friends taking classes in the *E Jing* and studying Wilber's *No Boundary,* I would not have stayed as long as I did.

However, one precious moment in a kindergarten classroom where I was teaching the *E Jing* made my year with them worthwhile. One night, I was scrawling all kinds of obscure symbols from the *E Jing* on the blackboard when suddenly everyone started laughing and asked me to go to the back of the class to look at the total scene. There were my ancient and profound Chinese characters and symbols surrounded by the permanent figures of Mickey Mouse, Donald Duck, and Dumbo etched into the blackboard, framing and putting my Earth-shattering revelations into perspective.

Teaching a Tai Ji class for the people in Tulsa also kept me there, plus the fact I was working only one hour a day. However, during the filming of *Rumble Fish,* they discovered I had healing ability, and that changed everything. From then on, it was 12-hour days for me.

One interesting development that came out of all that hard work was that I learned to heal without taking on the symptoms of others. I never had that problem in the short time I practiced acupuncture because the needles came between the client and me. When I switched to Chi Gung healing, I touched the patients directly and, as a result, I occasionally took on the symptoms of the people I was working with.

Because Chi Gung healing involves a more intimate mixing of energies with the client, I tried to cover myself with protective golden light while healing. I also did the "turbid chi" expulsion techniques after every treatment, etc., but I would still occasionally experience my patients' maladies. Some people's bioelectric energies were so gross that on a few occasions, it felt like hot, thick tar was going into my arms. This is why I suggest people not go into Chi Gung healing until they are strong, balanced, and clear.

It was also the huge number of people I saw in the course of a day that forced me to learn how to heal without harming myself. It was not unusual to work on 75 people in a single day. With numbers like that, my internal healing system quickly figured out how to survive such a large number of individuals. I not only learned how to protect myself, I was more energized at the end of the day than when I started. I had already spent years imagining the chi flow going out from my hands, and with practice, that flow felt stronger and more palpable. The chi flowing down through the top of my head through my arms and hands became so strong that it didn't allow a flow back. I actually benefited from the healings along with the clients. As my uncle used to say, "Necessity is a mother." Learning how to allow healing chi to flow through you unimpeded, without negative consequences, is one of those things you cannot teach. You can only learn it.

Also, in that healing period, I learned the importance of empowering the client. I gave everyone exercises and visualizations to do on their own. Most never did them, of course, but a few called me months later and said, for example: "That arm swing you showed me to lower my blood pressure has kept it down ever since." Many self-proclaimed healers tell me how many people they have cured, but when I ask them what techniques they give their patients to help themselves, they all look a little embarrassed and quickly change the subject. If you have a healer in your life that doesn't empower you to help yourself – find another healer.

Another unusual thing happened while I was with them. Because I had a lot of idle time on my hands, I often helped the crew do odd jobs. One day they were shooting a scene in a drive-in movie theater, and a storm started to blow.

It wasn't like any other storm I had seen before, but I was busily putting fake 1950 license plates over the real license plates of all the old cars the locals brought to the set. Even though the sky was turning a yellowish-gray, I didn't pay much attention to it until it started to sound like a freight train bearing down on me. Since I had never seen a tornado before, I didn't know what to do, so I ended up doing the dumbest thing possible. I took refuge in the circular popcorn stand; apparently, they are not the sturdiest buildings in the world.

The circular roof was sucked up. It flew through the air like a sickle, shearing off the tops of several vintage cars before lodging in the side of an immaculately restored pickup truck. As far as I know, no one was hurt. I got sucked upward a little but held tight to a railing. When the local owners of those classic cars returned to the drive-in after the storm, they cried their eyes out when they saw the damage to their cars. I later heard their cars were eventually restored.

Everyone asked if I was scared during it all, but I was so naive and so interested in what was going on, I forgot to be afraid. I actually stayed outside as long as I could to watch it. I could not imagine anyone not wanting to witness something that exciting. What I learned from all that is to head for the nearest basement when the sky turns a yellowish-gray, because curiosity did kill the cat, you know.

From Heaven to Purgatory Again

After nearly a year with the showbiz people, I decided in 1983 to retire at age 40 to one of my favorite spots on the planet, Taos, New Mexico. Talk about good topographical Feng Shui! That small, artsy-craftsy town is situated between a huge, 12,000-foot mountain to the east and a deep gorge of the Rio Grande River to the west. To experience those two powerful forces so close together is quite an experience. It is at their intersection where true creativity and power reside. There was skiing and astro-photography on the mountain in the fall and winter, and river rafting the Rio Grande gorge in the spring and summer.

I got a graphics job with a printing company designing brochures for the local artists and started a relationship with one of the artists. I was also a docent in the historic home of the famous Russian portrait artist Nicolai Fechin, who I still regard as being one of the great portrait artists of all time. I felt I had died and gone to heaven.

I was sure my Daoist teacher would visit and, upon sensing the energy there, insist on financing a Daoist center in the area – with me in charge, of course. Sure enough, a few years later, he came out for a weekend workshop, and ten minutes didn't go by before he commented on the powerful Feng Shui there.

As usual, he didn't exactly follow my fantasy. In fact, the next thing he said was, "Any fool can be in paradise and think they are enlightened. I want to see how you do in New York City." I said, "I hate New York." And he said, "That is all the more reason why you should experience it again."

A month later, in 1986, I was living in the shadow of the George Washington Bridge on the Upper West Side of Manhattan. There I was once again, back in "purgatory" after three years in "heaven." What a test of one's balance and peace of mind New York City was before 9/11. If you could maintain a sense of Play and oneness with the Universe there, to paraphrase the song, you could do it anywhere. Since I wanted to fulfill my teacher's wish to start a Daoist center there, I got a job in graphic design, started teaching classes in Tai Ji in Chinatown, and held Sunday morning services in my relatively large apartment.

Despite my resistance to New York City, as soon as I arrived, the synchronicities started happening on a daily basis. I noticed over the years that whenever I actually did what my teacher asked of me, I got deluged with synchronicities and good fortune. So, here is what happened in my first week in the city that never sleeps.

First, I was given a large apartment in the Cabrini Towers by one of my teacher's students. I put an ad in the local paper, and in just two days, I was already attracting students. One of them was

Margaret, a Jamaican princess who was the personal secretary to Harry and Leona Helmsley (owners of the Empire State Building!) She promised to introduce them to me but not until I got some decent clothes. I remembered seeing some clothes on the floor of one of the closets in my new apartment. Needless to say, the whole outfit fit like it was made for me!

Off we went to the Four Seasons restaurant. For you non-New Yorkers, the Four Seasons is not just a place to eat; it's a place to be seen. After a few minutes of being ignored because no one recognized us, suddenly everyone's attention turned to the elevator coming down from the penthouse. The owner of the restaurant walked out of the elevator and made a beeline for our table. He clicked his heels and kissed the back of Margaret's hand and said, "I heard you were in the building, so I just had to say hello." He then spun around and went back up the elevator, and for the next two hours, we had a hundred eyes staring at the two of us, trying to figure out who the hell we were!

So the moral of this story is...drum roll...if one is truly only on this Earth to help others, the Universe cannot help but resonate with them. I always say, be giving, open, and compassionate, and your life will be effortless. Unless, of course, you have a lesson to be learned, and even then, you will regard it as a blessing.

I still didn't like the city or most of the gross, obnoxious, aggressive people I met there. They were simply too much like me! However, one day my future wife walked through the door, and everything changed for me once again – even the city started looking better to me.

Marital Bliss, Divorce, and "Graduation"

It was a rare, cloudless day in New York when a good-looking woman came to my apartment and said, "I met your teacher when he passed through Indonesia last year, and I was so impressed with him I decided to follow him to the States." She wondered if she could study with me since he was no longer teaching. I said sure and asked her what she had learned in her nine years of living in Indonesia. She demonstrated Silat, a martial art originating in that part of the world, and showed me some spiritual practices their group had done. When she finished, I mustered all the tact and sensitivity I could at the time and told her she basically wasted nine years of her life learning that stuff. She promptly left in a huff, presumably never to be seen again.

Six months later, we ran into each other at our yearly Daoist meeting in Malibu. She told me my teacher had the same reaction to what she learned in Indonesia as I had, so she was now more receptive to what else I had to say about other things. The next thing I knew, it was 1989, and we were living together in Sacramento, "Californication," with her two children from a previous marriage. We then had a daughter of our own and decided to marry in 1990.

The term "culture shock" took on new meaning in my life. In a single year, I went from being a confirmed bachelor of 48 years to being a husband and father. It took quite an adjustment on my part. I can only imagine what my poor wife must have gone through. For starters, I have never had a desire to bring children into the world, considering the kind of future I saw ahead of us. To make matters worse, I was now responsible for three of them! My wife then exacerbated my bias by starting a preschool in our backyard to augment my salary.

Every day I returned home to a house full of ten snot-nosed, disease-carrying, obnoxious brats. It was about that time I found myself fantasizing about putting those children (excluding our three perfect children, of course) into a large, soundproof barrel with two small holes in it – one for feeding and one for waste products. (I exaggerate, of course. But only a little!)

Secondly, my attitude toward marriage was not exactly mainstream, either. I felt that living with the same person for a lifetime was biologically and psychologically unnatural, considering the different inherent needs and wants of the two genders and that our eternal souls eventually demand a wider love embrace. I have always had more of an impersonal compassion for people in general, rather than a love focus on any individual. I never actually "fell" in love; I was always dragged into it, kicking and screaming.

Thirdly, I wasn't even sure what love meant in those days, considering what people claiming to be in love were capable of doing to each other. The word is so overused! It is like an old coin that has been passed around so much it was rubbed blank until you can't tell its true worth anymore. For instance, how can a word that fits all of the following contexts have any meaning?

"I just love those shoes."

"I love the way you organized that lecture."

"I love you."

"I love it when you talk dirty to me."

"I love the acceptance I get in spiritual groups when I use the word 'love' in every sentence."

I seldom used the word, but when I did, it had more impact than when spoken by friends who used it frequently. My deepest and most lasting relationships seemed to be with people who shared my passion to help humanity spiritually evolve.

When two people share a common vision and look to it instead of each other to complete their fantasies or neuroses, the relationship has a better chance of lasting. When I discovered my future wife had roughly the same sentiments I did and that she was also attracted to Daoism and to my particular teacher, I jumped at the opportunity to spread "the gospel" with her. I figured our synergistic relationship could serve humanity more effectively than I could alone. That kind of thinking shows you how wrong I can be at times.

Despite my less than enthusiastic attitude toward marriage and children, I threw myself into being the best husband and father I could be. I simply regarded it as another opportunity to see how deeply rooted I was in my newly-evolving process of Play. I thought living in New York was a challenge – it paled in comparison to marriage.

I noticed pretty quickly that my usual state of impersonal compassion that worked well with my students had no impact on my kids. They demanded personal attention and love, and they wanted it NOW. It seemed like both the heaven and hell realms came in disguise as my family. But I am getting ahead of myself.

We began our blissful marriage with a beautiful Daoist Companionating Ceremony. If you are not familiar with Daoist weddings, here's my synthesis of several versions of how it is done.

The ceremony is usually performed in a gorgeous natural setting. Since I felt nature is overrated, we did it in the safe confines of our backyard. Even there, things were beyond our control. Our sprinkler system went off unexpectedly just before the ceremony, and we had to postpone the activities until it was fixed. How we missed that not-so-subtle message from the Universe is hard to believe.

Our guests entered to the sounds of Gregorian and Tibetan chanting. Everyone was given two flowers, one to wear and one to throw to us at the end of the ceremony. My seven-year-old stepson had the honor of striking a large gong nine times to start the ceremony. He missed the gong on his first swing, which was incredibly cute and set the tone for the rest of the proceedings.

The person performing the ceremony was Chao Li Chi, my Dao Duh Jing teacher from the Taoist Sanctuary in Los Angeles. He called on the guests to hold hands and form a circle of witness while celebrating with us. We then walked to four small altars situated in the four cardinal directions, where we invoked and honored the four elemental forces of the material world. (Earth, Air, Fire, and Water) We then returned to the Center altar (the fifth element holding the other four together) to proclaim our marriage a spiritual union. He then called upon us to nourish each other's highest physical, intellectual, and spiritual qualities and to be ever ready to inspire, instruct, encourage, and applaud each other for so long as our marriage should last.

The witnesses then threw flowers to us as we rushed off to a life of connubial bliss. This was so much better than "till death do us part."

Meanwhile, back to the "heaven and hell realms" of the marriage. After six months of our spreading the light of Daoism to the world, my wife announced, "I miss the social, communal aspects of my Jewish roots. I wonder if you would mind me returning to that tradition? Most Daoists are loners, and I need the sense of community that Judaism offers."

Okay, fine, I could accept that, being one with the universe and all, and considering my love embrace was infinite in scope. I even went to temple with her from time to time and socialized with her new Jewish friends. I found that I got along better with them than with my Christian friends because they don't take every word as "gospel." They spent a great deal of time discussing the meaning of various passages, so I fit in with them. Then she talked me into putting our kids into a private Jewish school. Okay, fine, it was a better education for the kids.

However, about a year later, during Shabbat, with them all reciting Hebrew and wearing their tzitzis, I put my foot down and announced I hadn't contracted for this and insisted on some changes. (So much for my infinite love embrace.) We agreed to home school our kids, which they all liked as long as they got to socialize with their new friends. My wife took up homeopathy as her new passion, and I didn't have to hear the sounds of ten screaming kids in the backyard anymore. I started teaching Tai Ji around the country on weekends, in addition to the four classes I had been doing daily. For the next six years, we were like two ships passing in the night.

With a routine like that, we slowly drifted apart. After seven years of marriage, we divorced. I am afraid our biggest problem was the fact that we suffered from irreconcilable similarities.

Most people I know describe their divorce as a living hell, but we seemed to escape most of that drama and pain. We both felt relieved, and I get along fine with her and her new husband. My sweet daughter visits me regularly, so I am content.

Not content to leave me content, my teacher had other ideas for me. This time he arranged for me to teach a group of his local and international teachers in Florida. I flew off to Florida to welcome them, all prepared to start a very intense three-day weekend with them.

The class was held in a large gymnasium, and just before it started, a phone on the floor rang. One of the women picked it up and said, "Hello?" and then, "Yes, I will tell everyone." When she hung up, she announced that Mark's teacher said to tell everyone that Mark is to leave immediately, and he never wants to see him or hear his name mentioned again! He added that Mark must never mention his teacher's name either. Since I had known most of these people for 20 years, you can imagine why the room got silent. Then everyone hugged me, and some cried. I told my assistant to take over and out the door I went!

My students obviously didn't know how "graduation" is celebrated in our sect. But I did, so I left without a fuss. And since I accepted the change with equanimity, I am sure he is proud of me. But that doesn't solve my next problem of what do I do now?

Here is a bit of a paradox: If upon hearing the news, I broke down in sorrow, rage, or resentment, it would have meant that he failed! Since I accepted the change with equanimity, I am sure he is quite proud of me. Although I have never been the "retiring" type, I decided maybe it was time for me to semi-retire, so I moved to Northern California to be near my daughter. And although I swore I would only feature my teachers in this book, I can't resist introducing my daughter because she is certainly one of my most formidable teachers!

MARITAL BLISS, DIVORCE, AND "GRADUATION" | 169

Below is Sita learning a new Tai Chi style, enjoying my 60th birthday party, and how she looks today. But I digress...onward to retirement!

Playing in Retirement

Looking out over the mountains from my lofty balcony in Northern California, I realize how content I am with my new, simplified Daoist life. I reduced my activities to selling Tai Ji DVDs, hosting tours to China and Tibet yearly, serving on the Advisory Committee to the National Qigong Association, conducting workshops around the country, and judging Tai Ji tournaments. In my "spare" time, I still do my astronomy thing, and flying ultralight planes has become my new transcendence practice. Nothing like the simple life of a Daoist, I always say. My wise uncle once commented on the way I live: "As I watch Mark manifest the great nothingness, I am reminded of how many necessities one can live without when one has enough luxuries."

Ultralight flying is not to be confused with what the knob-tweaking, "let's go somewhere," 150-miles-per-hour general aviation pilots do. We fly as God intended it. We get up in the air and putter along at 50 miles per hour a few hundred feet off the ground all day long, going no-where/now-here and loving every minute of it. One minute we are over the waves at the beach photographing whales, the next minute, we are throwing our shadows down on unsuspecting vehicles driving along the winding country roads. I get a big kick out of keeping my shadow on their hoods no matter which way they turn. They think I am a UFO, which is probably not far from the truth.

Ah, those moments of transcendence! Since my plane climbs like a homesick angel, I sometimes ascend to 10,000 feet (the maximum altitude we are allowed). I would then shut off the engine to soar around for 20 minutes with only the sound of the wind. I suspect that, for thousands of years, humans must have looked longingly at birds flying. So every time I fly, I say to myself, "This flight is for all you Neanderthals and Cro-Magnons who were longing to fly."

However, my Neanderthal uncle does not share that sentiment. He insists that if God wanted us humans to fly, he would have given us tickets. My daughter agreed with him after we hit a wet cow patty at one of my many "unscheduled stops" in a farmer's field.

In front of his plane, Mark, left, is interviewed by Adam Savage of the Discovery Channel's Mythbusters *series.*

It splattered all over her and the plane. If you are interested, try it (flying, that is...not landing in cowpies). All you have to remember is that when you pull back on the stick, the cows get smaller, and when you push it forward, the cows get bigger. We all have built-in parachutes in our planes, so they are much safer than they appear.

But I digress. Who has time to retire these days? All my 60- and 70-year-old friends are abuzz with partnering and collaboration. They say the era of individualism is over, and it is time to evolve the "we" space. Even business organizations are getting in on working together and supporting each other. I do not doubt that it is the next step in our evolutionary process, but can't we hold onto the "me space" just a little longer?

I gave up evolving years ago (all my friends will attest to that), and now I am supposed to evolve with others to help save the planet? The way I figure it, if Mother Earth survived the late Devonian, the Permian, and the Cretaceous extinctions, she doesn't need any help from me. Besides, how can I possibly get involved with all that "we" stuff now that I have discovered my hairline is receding!

I agree that we, as a species, have become a cancer to our planet, and we have become autistic in our lost capacity to communicate with the natural world. I also agree with eco-theologian Thomas Berry, who wrote, "We do not hear the voices of the trees, the rivers, the birds, the mountains, the animals, or the insects. We have become a death-dealing process. We judged progress by its benefits for ourselves."

On the other hand, I also feel that some of this nature-loving is overrated and for good reasons. I experienced frostbite at minus 20 degrees Fahrenheit in Pennsylvania when I was young. I suffered through two severe hurricanes in Florida, a tornado in Oklahoma, a devastating earthquake in Los Angeles, and a volcano in Hawaii. A mini-asteroid the size of a golf ball hit my trailer in

New Mexico, and none of that can match the horror of a mosquito or any crawling insect that manages to get into my apartment.

My nature-loving friends have all had natural botulism, natural intestinal parasites, and natural attacks by bee swarms. I think that much of the tree-hugging that is going on around me is a bit extreme. All I need in my simplified Daoist life is a temperature-controlled environment, 250 or more television channels, my plane, and thousands of adoring students. God knows I don't ask for much in life.

Not only do I think nature is often overrated, my estrangement from humanity has also been getting stronger. We warm-blooded, milk-sucking, overweight bags of stagnant fluids waddling around knee-deep in corn syrup and fructose seem mighty strange to me these days. Do you realize we humans are the laughingstock on this arm of the Milky Way galaxy?

With all our carefully tended hair strands sticking out from our bodies at various lengths, and those hideous, cauliflower-looking protrusions (ears) coming out the sides of our heads, along with our gimpy knees that were not designed to walk upright, and those funny-looking five toes sticking out from our long, weird, flat feet, it is no wonder the rest of the galaxy regards us as being rather strange. Can you imagine how badly humans must smell to other life forms? Between the bad breath, constant sweat, and horrible-smelling excrement, I am surprised we get close enough to each other to breed.

What a shock it must have been to the rest of the intelligent, intergalactic, asexual beings flying around in their UFOs when they discovered a hairy mammal had evolved to be the dominant species on this planet. No wonder they avoid contact with us. If we were reptilian, we would only have to eat once every month instead of eating everything in sight three times a day. Having sleek, cool, efficient bodies is a hell of a lot sexier than hot, hairy ones that smell bad.

My estrangement from humanity has me occasionally fantasizing about being an early scout sent from the Andromeda galaxy to warn all the intelligent Milky Way inhabitants of the Earth's impending collision with our galaxy. As you can imagine, my report on this particular solar system will have to be that no high intelligence exists here yet. If you don't believe this, just talk to people who only watch the Fox News channel. (I watch ALL news channels for greater overall perspective.)

However, you better get ready for the fireworks anyway. When Andromeda slices through the Milky Way, it is going to be really spectacular because it is nearly twice the size of our galaxy. It will happen in only two billion years or so, so start getting ready. I have no doubt some of you will still be reincarnating then, so put down those smart bombs and start organizing as a species and get out of this galaxy while you can.

Or, for a more accessible getaway, you can always travel to China.

Shangri-La

Playing in China and Tibet

Surely you don't think I spent my entire retirement flying around in small dangerous airplanes all day, do you? I soon became aware of how little Americans know about foreign countries in general, and China in particular, so I decided to take my students there on a yearly basis, and sometimes several times a year.

We usually fly directly to Beijing to visit the Great Wall and the Forbidden City, but due to the pollution and because Beijing is so crowded now, we don't stay more than a few days. Thanks to my business partner and all-purpose trip organizer, Rebecca Kali, we've had the extraordinary opportunity to visit people in their homes and learn about their daily lives. This has consistently been one of the highlights of our trips.

So after Beijing, we usually visited the Naxi and several other matriarchal communities in Southwest China, and in one town,

I got a firsthand look at how they live. The men sit in the center of town, smoking and talking all day, while the women plow the fields with babies perched on their backs from sunrise to sunset!

I am not exaggerating. The men live a life that has always been one of my fantasies...drinking and relaxing with my friends while the wives do all the work. The locals say, "every man wants a Naxi woman for his wife." I was hopeful some pretty Naxi woman would pick me, but no luck...so far.

From Beijing, we would fly directly to Chengdu in the southwest, then on to Chingcheng Shan, where we stayed in a 1,000-year-old temple guesthouse. Chengshan Shan is not only a gorgeous mountain, it is also the home of religious Daoism, founded by Zhang Daoling.

Of course, Daoism has prehistoric origins and was always more "spiritual" than "religious," but when Buddhism swept through China, Daoism was moved to organize and create the "Three Pure Ones" rituals, spirit healings, etc. Even with all of that, Daoists have never been a major spiritual influence in China.

My latest observation is that China's major religion now seems to be: emulating the U.S.A! One day I asked why all the billboards used Americans to sell things, and they said: "Since you have all the goodies on the planet, when you promote something, it must be the best available!" In other words, they are getting as materialistic and superficial as we are.

In contrast, we also went out of our way to experience Shangri-La. It is just as beautiful and magical as James Hilton described in his famous book, *Lost Horizon*. After several days in this lofty paradise, we would fly to Lhasa, Tibet.

We have also never been disappointed by our experiences in Tibet. Short bus rides brought us to the foot of the Himalayas with jaw-dropping scenery along the way. There were yaks to ride everywhere, and to our surprise, pool tables were found in the most

PLAYING IN CHINA AND TIBET | 179

remote areas you can imagine. Not to mention Buddhist monks debating philosophy in the parks. I actually joined the fray once, and they all asked me to return (to America, no, just kidding). But the biggest attraction was and still is the Potala, the Dalai Lama's winter palace when he lived in Tibet. It has over 1,000 rooms and a panoramic view of 50 miles in all directions.

Don't get the idea it was all sweetness and light for me. Every morning I led Tai Chi and Qigong classes, and every night we learned a new aspect of Daoism. While my students were immersed in self-healing and the mysteries of the *E Jing,* and absorbed in nightly readings of the *Dao Duh Jing,* and practicing calligraphy with a brush, it was the afternoon strolls that wore me out! Have you ever tried to herd 15 people up a modest incline at 15,000 feet only to learn halfway up, they forgot their oxygen bottles? Many of you may not know that when you have fifteen potential Daoists discuss ANY subject, you can be sure there will be at least eighteen perspectives on the matter! Oh, how I suffered!

Okay, I have to admit, leading these trips every year and taking a great group of like-minded people with me is not really such a bad way to retire! So, enjoy the trip photos above and dream about joining us on an amazing adventure. Meanwhile, back to our present reality...the biggest challenges facing humanity!

The Biggest Challenges Facing Humanity

This chapter is divided into three parts. The first discusses the need to understand the Yin/Yang symbol and the theory behind it because it is a visual code to the foundation of everything, and very few people understand it. The second is looking at the need to learn how to integrate our "shadows" or the subconscious content of our being. Until that is done, we will continue to project our repressed fears and rage onto others. The third is the need to understand if everyone is striving to be happy all the time, then why isn't there more happiness in the world?

Because these three points are closely related to each other, it means that if we do not make some progress soon on all three fronts, it could lead to the collapse of our civilization, if not the extinction of our species. How much longer can we continue to equate success with destroying our environment while greedily accumulating as many goodies as possible at the expense of everyone else? So, let's get to work with addressing these three points and get on with our evolution on all levels.

Point #1. *The need to understand the Yin/Yang symbol.* There is a lot more to the Yin/Yang symbol than meets the eye.

Many people do not see the inner connectedness of it. Most people do not understand how this united force manifests in the dualistic world, and fewer still actually utilize the deep implications of this little symbol. As a result, not many people are capable of Play as I have defined it throughout this book.

Let me explain.

Have you noticed I do not refer to the symbol as the Yin AND Yang symbol? *That is because they are two inseparable parts of the same whole.* Similarly, the two small dots that look like the eyes of two "tadpoles" are implying that the seed of yang is contained in the yin and vice versa. Furthermore, *when one aspect is pushed to its limit, it will become the other.*

Another thing to notice is its shape, which indicates constant movement and change while circling toward each other. If these were two separate entities, they would be divided by a straight line. In other words, this symbol is a picture of energy that oscillates between the two bandwidths of *itself.*

The four visuals on the next page reflect the different approaches to living in a dualistic world that isn't all that dualistic.

Below is a visual representation of the "Wu Chi" (before duality). It is represented as a "flat line" or stillness on the screen of an oscilloscope. When the oscilloscope is still, it is one. With no movement, there can be no sense of time or duality. When waves are created, they differ in speed, direction, and size. Their separate qualities indicate the birth of duality. A few meditators I know only want this – a perfectly still mind beyond time and space. Why incarnate if that is all you want? And if you see this on your oscilloscope in the hospital, you will know you only have seconds to live!

Below are the first perceptible ripples on a still pond. This first, subtle movement is like intergalactic beings that have evolved beyond physicality over billions of years into a universal field of consciousness. They are incredibly subtle light/dark beings and are the first manifestations of duality to emerge from the great Oneness.

Below is the gently rolling wave curve of all highly-evolved sages on this planet. They are not as subtle in their beings as the ones above, but they are much more subtle and evolved than nearly everyone else on this planet. But hey, I am willing to cut us some slack because we only crawled out of the trees a mere five million years ago!

The next image is what the energy of a manic-depressive looks like. They spend most of their time and energy striving for bliss and trying to feel good all the time until they find themselves in a self-created dark pit of depression with no energy, wondering how they got there.

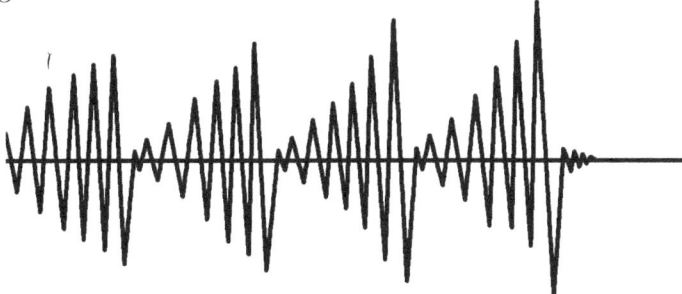

If that last energetic picture is indicative of your present energetic state – moderate your life. Allow the natural processes of nature to gently flow you. If you think you know the difference between what is good for you and what isn't, here's a story to contemplate.

A long time ago in China, there lived a wise old man who had only two possessions: his horse and his son. He was loved and revered by everyone in his village, so on the day his stallion ran away, all the townspeople came out to commiserate with him. To their surprise, he wasn't the least bit upset. In fact, he said, "I don't know whether my horse running away was a good thing or a bad thing. It simply happened."

Since the old man could no longer plow his fields without his horse, everyone took up a collection of food for him. However, the next day, his horse returned with several wild mares, making him the wealthiest person in the village. As the villagers were exclaiming about what a wonderful thing it was that the horse returned with the mares, he again calmly said, "I don't know if having all these horses is a good thing or a bad thing. It simply happened."

They returned home shaking their heads, wondering how he failed to see the good in it all. The next day, while breaking in one of the mares, his son fell off one of them and broke his leg in three places, rendering him disabled for life. This time the villagers were convinced the old man would see the horror in his son being disabled, but all he said was, "I don't know if his being disabled is a good thing or a bad thing. It simply happened."

That was more than they could comprehend. They thought he had lost his mind until the next day when the local army came through the village and gathered up all the able-bodied boys and men to go on a suicide mission.

Because of his broken leg, the farmer's son was the only one spared. After that, the villagers became more hesitant to label something as being obviously good or bad.

Something else that has shifted my attitude on this subject has been meeting numerous cancer survivors, who concluded, "If I hadn't gotten cancer, I would still be superficially sailing along on the surface of life. Because of the cancer, I have been forced to do some deep self-reflection on the meaning of my life and death, and as a result, I now only focus on matters of real consequence to me."

The meaning of all this is not to say we should sit around and passively accept everything that happens to us. The wise old man was being true to himself. If you feel something is intolerable, then be true to yourself and act on that feeling.

Being authentically who we are at all stages of our growth (with plenty of room to expand and evolve) is another foundation of a life of Play.

Another important aspect of Yin/Yang profundity is the fact that *we in the West have been incorrectly taught that "good" will eventually triumph over "evil" – by eliminating it!* And I know of no better way to point out the folly of that thinking than to contrast the mythical flood stories of the West with the flood stories of China.

In ancient times, both the eastern Mediterranean and China experienced great floods, but the perspectives and the reactions of the people in these two areas were completely different. The people of the eastern Mediterranean mostly lived in desert areas with not much more than sun and sand to inspire them. Because their environment was so stark, they tended to think in terms of black and white to the point that they actually conjured up a mythical god that tried to use force to eliminate all the "bad" people of the world. That myth became a basic element of the psyches of the people who practiced Judaism, Christianity, and Islam.

As the Judeo-Christian story goes, Yahweh (God) decided to wipe out the entirety of the evil human race except for those he deemed "good." Fortunately for Noah and his family, they were on his "chosen" list. Yahweh obviously didn't understand Yin/Yang theory, or he would have never pulled that stunt; because what did it get him? Within a few generations or less, humans were back to being as evil as ever!

On the other hand, we can look at China to see a completely different way of dealing with "evil." After one "evil" flood followed another, the Great Yu, as he was later called, set out to do something about it. Apparently, he was a student of Yin/Yang theory because he got his large, extended family to spend decades cutting channels out of the rocks. The channels redirected the floods away from the villages and towns, and the people used the water to irrigate the fields. His method worked, and incidentally, his crude, ancient channels are still visible today.

The Daoists have always said that any powerful force is simply energy to use, *whether you classify it as good or evil and whether it originates within yourself or from the outside world.* In fact, that perspective is now the foundation of Tai Ji and Aikido, both of which grew out of the understanding of Yin/Yang theory. My Chinese teacher often said: "There is no reason for fear because if you know how to redirect powerful energies, your life and the lives of everyone around you will be safer and more peaceful."

I have one last example of how to use Yin/Yang energy, but before relating it, I feel compelled to issue a warning: if you do not understand the subtle workings of Yin/Yang interaction, then don't try this at home! I once watched my teacher redirect the energy of a natural cycle in his life that he didn't like, and I will never forget it. Here's the story.

One hot summer day, my teacher complained he hadn't had a patient in two days, nor a girlfriend in months, and that his house had been on the market for over a year without selling. I said I was sorry to hear that and went back to editing books. A few minutes later, he yelled out, "Get me the donkey gall bladders that are in a jar in my herb room!" It wasn't long before he was cutting and frying them in the kitchen. The smell was so bad, those of us in the house at the time took our work outside to the other end of his property. Even at that distance, we still gagged occasionally. Only after several hours did we feel safe to go back inside.

The next day, a good-looking female patient arrived, and he left with her for the day. When he returned 24 hours later, he happily announced he had just sold his house to her. His girlfriend problem was apparently also solved. I was interested in learning how he turned that cycle around so fast, but he wouldn't tell me because he didn't want me to try it. However, here is what I surmised he did.

He was in a natural cycle of the flow of Yin/Yang that probably would have lasted for several more months, but he was unwilling to wait that long for it to run its course. I suspect he ate bitter food to an extreme in order to experience the "sweet" in a hurry. Conversely, you have to admit that when one eats sweet to excess, one then quickly experiences the bitter task of having to live with diabetes. He knew that if you push yin or yang to its extreme, it will reverse itself, and he obviously had the "gall" to demonstrate it!

Of course, he had 50 years to perfect that skill. If I had tried it, my results would have been a trip to the hospital to get my stomach pumped out. Then I would have experienced more bitterness when the bill came due. Since I was taught as a Zen Buddhist "to go with the flow," my Daoist friends remind me that we have the spark of the creator within us, and it is okay to try manipulating our reality if we know what we are doing. Unfortunately, most of us don't.

In summation then, Yin/Yang is literally the "open secret" or code of "reality," the use of which makes you efficacious whether you chose to go with the flow or change it as you see fit.

Point #2. *The need to integrate our shadow.* This is one of the more serious challenges facing humanity. By shadow, I mean the 70 to 90 percent of our being that is not under our conscious control or even awareness. We humans are similar to icebergs in that the greatest percentage of our mass and energy is below the surface. Our conscious lives are like the small part of the iceberg that is above water. This part is much less influential in determining where the iceberg floats than does the mass of the iceberg below the surface due to the strong oceanic undercurrents directing it. Therefore, positive thinking and visualizing things does very little to determine what life brings us if our subconscious is not included.

Because of our unwillingness to face and integrate our subconscious content, we humans have powerful unseen energies that sabotage our aspirations, relationships, societies, governments, educational and banking systems, and of course, our healthcare system. All these aspects are affected because if everyone is either not recognizing or suppressing their fears, rage, shame, pain, and guilt, those repressed energies will eventually erupt – unless they are integrated and transformed. They do not like being relegated to the cellar any more than our strange uncle enjoyed being locked down there. (Just kidding.)

On the mundane level, most people walk around quite unaware of the fact they even have a subconscious. *As a result, they end up projecting it out onto others without knowing it is their own energy.* Some of it is and always will be subconscious, but much is repressed parts of ourselves that we can't or won't integrate. Actually, most of our unrecognized energy turns out to be our own unrecognized self-created drives.

One example from my life was when I announced I was going out to wash the car. An hour later, my wife saw me sitting next to it, reading a magazine, and innocently said, "Oh, I thought you were going to wash the car, dear." I then responded, "Get off my back – you are always pushing me!" The truth was, there was no pressure coming from her. It was all an unrecognized inner drive of my own that I projected onto her. If I had been aware of my own need to clean the car – or in this case, not clean the car – I would have simply admitted I changed my mind and decided to read the magazine instead. Don't get the idea I am saying that wives never put pressure on husbands – God knows I would never insinuate that!

Another example of unrecognized energy is our "Inner Critic" (usually the echo of a judgmental parent) – the part of us always undermining our self-confidence. It can make a person feel depressed, inadequate, ashamed, guilty, etc., even though it is actually trying to prevent any future failures in whatever one undertakes. It needs to be engaged and slowly transformed into the truly helpful ally it can be. If you suspect your shadow is sabotaging your life, do not put off ignoring the elephant in your living room that has been sabotaging the conversation.

While some of our subconscious content is a result of repression, a lot of our fear and pain comes from the DNA of our parents or even our past lives (If you don't believe in past lives, don't worry. You will in your next lifetime). Those energies are so deep and powerful that talk therapies are often ineffective with them. Like the time my wounded inner child came out in a talk session, and my inner warrior came out and killed him. (Just kidding, again.) There truly are powerful forces that cannot be touched by any amount of talk therapy. However, certain Daoist breathing exercises can expel any energetic force stunting our lives. What's more, you do not have to utter a word for the exercises to work.

When we saturate our system with large amounts of chi through our rapid, deep breathing, it eventually "blows out" any energetic blockage hindering the natural flow. The results are much more dramatic than the "chaotic meditation" mentioned earlier. People would spasm uncontrollably; others would scream they hated their parents, and eventually, there would be a lot of crying. This is not for the faint-of-heart and should be done only with a master.

However, Stanislav Grof has created a similar technique called Holotropic Breathwork. Find a certified practitioner of his system and release all the inner horrors plaguing you from birth and beyond. When those energies are released, they can be transformed into helpers, and you will soon experience the shadow working for you rather than against you. What do you think my story about the bear chasing me was all about?

Nowadays, I notice that most psychiatrists are all too content with drugging their patients out of their minds so that they don't feel a thing rather than getting to the cause of their pain. Meanwhile, many of my spiritual friends won't touch their rage, fear, or pain with the proverbial 10-foot pole either. They believe there's no problem in life that meditation won't cure. Yet, meditation does not cure deep unconscious blockages. It is great for many other things, but we must first integrate our shadow. If we don't, the shadow will sabotage any spiritual insights we might gain through meditation. Constant meditation is like getting on a fast elevator in a tall building crumbling around you. *How many corrupt gurus or priests do we have to endure, and how much personal failure do we have to go through before we are willing to dive into our pain and hidden agendas and grow from the experience?*

Point #3. *What happens to a Civilization that lives only to be "happy" all the time?* For most people, that means having all Yang and no Yin! So many people live only to be "happy." If that is the case, then why isn't happiness more prevalent in the world today? Why is there an epidemic of anxiety and depression?

Making matters worse, we have technologies that make instant gratification possible. Only a hundred years ago, our technological discoveries were geared toward feeding and clothing ourselves, whereas technology today can instantly fill our every want. To exacerbate the problem, too many people confuse their selfish wants with their true needs. If we made helping others our first priority, we would all be happier!

Hence, we have given birth to several generations of impulsive people, who've become completely intolerant of physical or psychological discomfort. This leads to a greedy, self-destructive perspective incapable of long-range planning. Impulsive psyches explain how in 2008, the financial industry gambled with trillions of dollars until it nearly caused a worldwide financial meltdown.

The industry encouraged mortgage companies to issue loans to people they knew would never be able to pay them back. Even our politicians are willing to shut down the government with their games of partisan risk-taking to get what they want. The top "one percent" is willing to suck the life out of the poor and middle class until no one is left to consume. Need I go on? It is bad enough we are willing to do all that to ourselves, but what are we doing to the environment? How can we secure a future for our children and ourselves when people and institutions are hell-bent in the pursuit of ever-narrowing self-interest?

Experiments show that the people best suited for success in life are capable of self-restraint and delayed gratification. You may be aware of the "marshmallow test" as an indicator of future success in life. A five-year-old is given a marshmallow and told that if he doesn't eat it until the adult returns to the room, he will be given a second marshmallow. They found that only a very small percentage of children are capable of waiting, and follow-up studies indicate that those who can wait end up being the most successful people in life.

It is also obvious to me that those who are the most comfortable working with both their conscious and subconscious aspects are the healthiest, most authentic, and whole people I know. It is only by learning to embrace and use so-called negative emotions, as well as so-called positive ones, can we access ALL our energies that help us cope with the vicissitudes of life. I am convinced that our spiritual treasure and portal to complete integration depends upon this most important undertaking. But don't "mis-underestimate" me: I think it is a good thing when thinking positively and being optimistic can get you out of the hole of thinking negatively.

However, if blind optimism is pursued without letup, it will become an extreme, and like any other extreme, it will reverse itself. By accepting the challenge of drawing on the dark side when appropriate, you bring wholeness and light into your lives.

I know of no group of people who need this advice more than the many spiritual seekers I meet these days. Robert Augustus Masters, in his book *Spiritual Bypassing*, also makes the same point that people use spiritual beliefs to avoid dealing with painful feelings, unresolved wounds, and developmental needs. He says, "They say spirituality will give them immunity from pain and all the other troublesome matters of life – what a fantasy! Spirituality ultimately means no escape, no need for escape, and utter freedom through limitation and every sort of difficulty."

To reiterate, I want you to know that the Yin/Yang symbol tells us we do NOT evolve from yin to yang or from dark to light – we evolve from gross Yin/Yang to subtle Yin/Yang and beyond – which includes them both.

I want to emphasize the need for moderation in all things because if we don't, we will all eventually end up on the rapidly expanding bandwagon of extremist manic-depressives. Once you have the extremes in your life moderated, it is time to integrate your shadow. If you don't, that aspect of yourself will sabotage everything you try to do in life. The good news is if you DO integrate it, it becomes a powerful ally.

To summarize, unless we address our civilization's crippling blind spots – the misunderstanding of Yin/Yang; the failure to integrate the shadow; the blind pursuit of what we imagine to be "happiness" through instant gratification – there will come a time when the majority of us will live impulsively and be incapable of any mature long-range planning...and we will self-destruct.

This leads beautifully to one of my favorite subjects – death.

Playing with Death and Immortality

Whether you believe there is nothingness when you are dead, favor the Christian idea of heaven and hell, or prefer the Eastern concept of reincarnation, here's what to expect. There is no need to fear nothingness because there is no such thing as hell, pain, conflicts, or obstacles of any kind in nothing. Being the absence of everything, there will be nothing to fear, and no one there to do the fearing.

Forget about pearly gates, streets lined with gold, winged angels with perfect, immortal bodies singing the praises of God forever. That squeaky-clean sameness sounds more like hell to me because I like novelty. Besides, any God who craves praise and threatens to torture me for eternity if I don't praise Him is no God I want to know – especially now that we have other choices.

A mere hundred years ago, very few people knew anything about other religions, but nowadays, there is no excuse to stay ignorant of other people's points of view. I happen to get great pleasure from helping people get over their ignorance and fears, but in the Western version of Heaven, I would be out of a job because everyone is perfect up there.

Here is what I have gathered about the afterlife so far. Just head for the light at the end of the tunnel, and you will be fine. Loved ones or a guide of some kind will greet you. Christians sometimes see Jesus, Buddhists see the Buddha, and so on. According to which frequency you are capable of, you will gravitate naturally to the level of "heaven" or "hell" you resonate with. Don't panic, they are all temporary.

Working out your good or bad karma is not an eternal punishment. *What kind of a God punishes someone eternally for something done in a finite lifetime?* Our present laws decree that we should punish in accordance with the nature of the crime. The notion that we come into being to live one, short, tragic life to be rewarded with heaven, or condemned to hell for eternity, is mythical nonsense perpetuated to control children. We are not children. We must start becoming adults of God. Why continue holding on to such immature and unsubstantiated ideas when the reality of birth and death is so much more interesting?

After a quick life review and a brief intermission in the heaven or hell you deserve, you will find yourself right back here. Your life trajectory will simply continue where you left off in the last one. That is why killing yourself is a waste of time. You will reap what you sow. So be more careful about what you sow.

What I am trying to emphasize here is that you have a choice in this lifetime. You can plant seeds that benefit yourself and humanity and live in peace and harmony forever, or you can choose to be selfish and destructive and live in misery. (Hint – choose the former and not the latter) Either way, you will inevitably reap in the next lifetime what you sowed in this lifetime. (More details on reincarnation in the next chapter.)

Now, let's talk about immortality. Lately, I have had several occasions to prove my immortality to my friends and students. Over twenty years ago, a car going 40 miles per hour hit me in a crosswalk, and I left the scene without even a scratch. I was walking along, minding my own business (which is everything), and all of a sudden, my cat-like reflexes made me jump four feet into the air!

I had no idea why – it was a reflex I had cultivated in training. I didn't see or hear anything, and the driver obviously didn't see me because he never hit his brakes until after he saw me flying in the air. Usually, when a human body and a car collide, it is bad for the body. But if you do the lower-vortex practices shown in this book and have 40 years to build a chi shield around you, there is a good chance you too might escape such a collision with minor damage.

The top of his windshield sent me another five feet into the air, but I landed on his roof, which absorbed my fall. I was carrying my DVD sales for the day, and all the white bubble mailers went flying along with me. The crowd that gathered said it looked like a meteorite shower. A doctor in the crowd insisted on me taking an ambulance to the hospital only three blocks away. When I found out there were no broken bones, I decided to walk home. I couldn't even find a bruise on me the next day. It is a good thing I had many witnesses, or I wouldn't have believed it myself. Okay, that was spectacular and dramatic, and I milked it for all the attention I could get, but what followed was the real deal.

About a year later, I was about to go flying when I discovered my engine was running rough, so I decided to fly with someone I had never flown with before. Remind me to never do that again!

All I remember is getting in his plane and then waking up in the intensive care unit three days later. Apparently, we lost power on takeoff, flew through a fence, and hit a warehouse.

How anyone survived that crash is a miracle. But, hey, if I am not involved in at least one miracle by noon every day, I feel I've

What was left of the plane afer they cut us out of it.

wasted my morning. The pilot only had a few cuts and bruises because his seat belt held, while mine ripped loose from the frame of the plane. I demolished his instrument panel with my face as I flew through his windshield, and my right leg was broken in three places.

After a day of facial reconstruction and another operation for a fractured leg, I was as fit as an old, badly damaged fiddle. This looked worse than it was. When I woke up, I had no memory of the crash, nor any pain. I did not need to take a pain pill during rehab. However, they told me I was paranoid as hell after I woke up, probably due to the powerful drugs they gave me to keep me in an induced coma until my facial swelling went down. I was convinced they were trying to kill me, so I yanked the tubes out of my throat and arms and tried to run away. I didn't get very far. The titanium plates and 48 stitches in my leg severely limited my ability to crawl down the hallway.

In spite of my non-cooperative attitude, they said I healed like an 18-year-old. Considering my ex-wife insisted I acted like a 15-year-old most of the time she knew me, I consider that progress. After two weeks in the hospital and another week in rehab, it only took two months of rehab at home to be teaching Tai Ji again.

So why didn't I die, and how did I heal so fast, and what have I learned from it all? During the missing three days in that coma, I remember shouting, "Where is the light at the end of the tunnel? Isn't there supposed to be a goddamn light around here somewhere?" The doctors later told me my vital signs were always strong, so there was no near-death experience. I now realize a disadvantage of being an "immortal" is not having any near-death experiences to brag about!

Here's how I healed so fast. I allowed it to happen by being still and letting my body do its work. I figured my body knows what it needs better than I do, so I allowed it to do its thing. Also, when one lives the kind of lifestyle I do, one gets good at healing fast.

All my friends wanted to know why this happened and what I learned from it. I learned the same thing from it I do from every experience I now have – nothing. When I was young and foolish, I used to think everything happened for a reason and that we are here to learn and grow. That might be valid for those who think they are pre-enlightened individuals, but it doesn't apply to post-enlightened beings. Keep in mind that a part of you is already post-enlightened, so get used to the idea.

Somewhere along the space-time continuum, I Playfully fell off the endlessly revolving hamster wheel of self-improvement and striving for things. I am not sure when that happened. I only became aware of that transition through hindsight because my life evolved pretty much as before. Only now, I don't labor under the illusion I am solely in charge here. As Ramana Maharshi once said, "You are like people riding in a train with your baggage on your head!" I usually add, "While you complain about having a stiff-neck."

THE NINTH IMMORTAL

The newest and obviously best-dressed Immortal of the bunch.

The ride will continue, so put down your personal baggage and enjoy it. In other words, Play.

By experiencing life as Play and demonstrating my immortality, I now qualify to join the Daoist Eight Immortals Club. (As the comedian Stephen Wright said, "I am going for immortality. So far, so good.") Until now, the Daoists have revered eight individuals who they claim keep reappearing throughout history, so they must be immortal. It is about time they recognized one more person. Too bad they will have to redraw and rewrite all their scrolls and scriptures, but you have to admit Nine Immortals sounds more complete than eight. On the next page is my proposed redrawing of the Nine Immortals Club. It will soon appear on my very own "Ascended Master Card."

If I happen to be wrong about being an immortal and if this fuzzy bag of bacteria I've lived in since 1942 turns out to be like mere mortals who die and come back again, please scatter my ashes in outer space in the direction of Andromeda and put this sign on the urn: *"To be continued...or maybe not."*

Be sure to add: "RETURN TO SENDER!"

Playing
with Reincarnation

If you have no memories of your past lives, I suggest you read Dr. Ian Stevenson's research on the subject. I still regard his research as being the most professional, congruent, and credible. He investigated over 2,800 cases of children who "remembered" past lives. His evidence is not merely the recording of some children's fantasies. He only investigated those cases with a wealth of details that he and his staff could research to see if they were accurate or not. He even took children back to visit the families they claimed to have come from in their previous lives. Several murder cases in India were solved when the murderer was confronted with the testimony a child who had been the murder victim in a recent previous life! Ian has written many books on the subject, and they are all fascinating.

From my readings, and more importantly, from my own experiences, I regard reincarnation as simply the way the Universe works.

Without the "big picture" that reincarnation affords, you miss the deep interconnection your life has with that of the Universe.

Just as a wave has complete access to the entirety of the Ocean, it is possible to have memories of when you were a mammal, a bird, a fish, a reptile, a one-celled creature, a molecule, an atom, or even back to the Big Bang. This view – that humans evolved from lower forms of life (called transmigration) – is not as far-fetched as it sounds. The following examples will show why.

Did you know that several times a century, a human is born with quite a few digits of a tail? Our tails, from when we were primates, are in our present DNA and, therefore, still in our cellular memories. In most people, that tail DNA is turned off because tails are no longer useful to us. Those babies born with the stunted tails didn't have those parts of their DNA turned off, so they actually had to have operations to remove the vestigial tails.

I saw a program on the Discovery Channel recently that showed how scientists turned on the DNA of the tail and teeth of an ostrich, even though that bird hasn't had a tail or teeth since it was a dinosaur. The scientists said that it is only a matter of a few years until they can recreate the ancestors of all living creatures by re-activating their dormant genes.

We have all evolved from the simple to the complex with greater capacities for cooperation and unity. What force brought atoms together to form molecules? What force united molecules to become a strand of DNA? What force united the strands of DNA into cells, and then into organs, and then into people, and what attracted people to unite in communities? *It was the power of LOVE... the drive toward unity and cooperation.*

But don't swoon over this fundamental force of Nature because there is an equal force called Entropy that does the opposite. It makes all things fall apart over time. Let a perfectly good Mercedes car sit around too long in your driveway, and it will disintegrate into a pile of rust.

In addition to the physical evidence of our long evolution, there are psychological benefits to accepting reincarnation as a fact. Have you noticed how people who have had near-death experiences and/or memories of reincarnation dramatically change after having had such an experience? They become much more loving and fearless. Read about their experiences and know for yourself that:

Life is eternal.
You have as many lifetimes to perfect yourself as you want and need.

Death loses its sting when you are convinced you have multiple lives to perfect yourself. When you are fearless, you are less easily manipulated by the fearmongers of every age. One of the more obvious and crude examples of manipulating with fear is the notion that you have only one life to live, and then you must face the possibility of eternal damnation.

I hope you no longer need those scare tactics to be good anymore. When people are secure in the knowing and the experience that they are never separated from the eternal, recurring source of life, they cannot be easily manipulated.

The notion that we come back as some lower life form if we are "bad" is also ridiculous and not supported by the evidence. *We are born out of unfulfilled desires,* so if you spent your entire last life playing Tchaikovsky on the piano and not doing much else, you could very well be reborn a savant and end up on some talent show. I am also sure that coming back as a cockroach would not satisfy the needs of a classical pianist.

Reincarnation is also the only logical explanation for the inequality of births. If we have only one life to live, why would a loving and just God create a crack baby in a ghetto to die young after experiencing only misery and violence most of its life, while another baby is born into a loving family with all kinds of material and spiritual advantages?

The role of pain and suffering in people's lives is also best understood and appreciated in the larger context that reincarnation provides. Pain is the great liberator that pushes most people to transcend their small lives.

If everything always goes smoothly, then why would anyone ever evolve? Pain is actually a Portal through which we remember who we really are.

That is why all highly evolved psychologists and spiritual people say to go into your pain instead of taking toxic drugs to numb yourself against it. Avoiding your psychological pain only makes things worse in the end.

Of course, if you are in great physical pain, then pain relief is appropriate. But I assure you, if you dive deep into your pain – and I am not referring to suffering, which is what you conjure up as the result of true pain – you will come out of it with a more expanded view of your true self and of all lives.

If we do not have multiple lives to work things out, then the wise saying, "You reap what you sow," is a lie because many bad people go unpunished in their current lifetime. In my opinion, that proverb about reaping what you sow is one of the fundamental principles of life and death. This has also been called "the law of karma."

I hear that many psychologists are still arguing over whether nature or nurture is the driving force in most people's lives. I think those two possibilities are only two-thirds of the equation. If you only consider those two factors, they do not explain why identical twins often lead such diverse lives. Twins share the same DNA and get the same nurture from their family, so why the vast difference in aspiration, direction, and outcome of their lives? I think that what we bring with us from previous lives mostly determines what happens to us. There is certainly no DNA way to explain me!

Finally, I discovered what I think is the most significant aspect of reincarnation. I found it in Ian's Stevenson's *Where Reincarnation and Biology Intersect*. Out of the 2,800 cases he investigated, he amassed photographic evidence on 225 cases that show birthmarks and scars on the young children that corresponded to the stories they told about how they died or were killed. While interesting in itself, that evidence has deep and fascinating implications.

What those photographs imply is that the incoming soul is capable of overriding the DNA of the biological parents. Most of their birthmarks faded with age but, for a while, the soul seemed to be capable of creating discernible marks on the body until the DNA of the parents took over. This fact might explain an answer my Chinese teacher gave me once when I asked him if we could change our DNA with Chi Gung, Tai Ji, and meditation. He said. "To the extent you are identified with, and manifest your higher self, you can change and influence anything."

In my opinion, reincarnation is a major force behind most of our lives. The Universe changes and renews itself through repetitive cycles and evolves from the simple to the complex over billions of years. So do we. Read Ian Stevenson and others. The evidence is overwhelming.

Playing with Enlightenment

I promised to explain why striving for enlightenment is futile and why not striving for it is also futile. It is difficult to discuss enlightenment in general because enlightenment means something different to everyone and because it is paradoxical. Most people think enlightenment is a peaceful, blissful, formless realm beyond the manifest world and outside of space and time. This is only partially correct because it is a paradox.

It is paradoxical because enlightenment includes duality and is simultaneously beyond it.

A lot of people who study Eastern religions are busily quieting their minds and emotions and are waiting for "enlightening" to strike. This is what the Buddha and Shankara taught and what I meditated on for almost 20 years. I have friends who are professional meditators. They can sit without a single thought appearing in their minds for hours at a time. However, I have rocks in my backyard that can do the same thing. Is this the apex of life on this planet? *The Oneness as Emptiness is only part of the story. The manifest realm is also an expression of the great Oneness.* Our task now is to figure out how best to manifest that ground of being in the evolving, material world. We must merge the transcendent with the immanent.

The analogy of the Ocean with its waves is the best way I know to describe the paradox of being both at the same time. Waves provide a good analogy for people because each wave has a discernible, separate existence. Each has a unique size, direction, speed, and shape – and they make a lot of noise, just as I do! There is also no real separation between them and the totality of the Ocean.

So imagine yourself as an average wave rolling along, minding your own business, and some guru wave tells you, "You are the entirety of the ocean, and you can experience yourself as such." All you have to do is meditate your ass off, become a vegetarian, and take up Tai Ji, or, if you are the trusting, devotional type, you can surrender to Yahweh, Jesus, or Allah.

So now they become a seeker with a mission! A wave in search of wetness! Nothing like a little meaning in life to actually get a person to do something other than consume stuff to compensate for that endless dark pit of need in the middle of one's chest. The fanatic edge that sometimes comes with a little meaning in one's life can drive a seeker for several thousand lifetimes; in spite of a few setbacks such as exhaustion, depression, and the sneaky feeling you are wasting a lot of time.

Some people start wave hopping to find the wetness, and others start perfecting their own wave to get wetter than the other waves. What keeps that cycle going is the fact that every time someone gets weary, another spiritual teacher comes along with the perfect technique for experiencing wetness, and off they go again until they finally drop. And then, "POW," a moment of unity consciousness.

If you stop striving for wetness in order to succeed in experiencing it, it will not work. *You have to stop everything, which includes stopping everything.* That is why not too many people actually do it. It is scary to surrender everything you think you are and allow the great Oneness to continue running the show.

Some of the best "strivers" I have ever met are the Zen folks. They tirelessly scale that "enlightenment" mountain going straight up the slopes, while most people meander around the well-worn paths, smelling the flowers and eating the strawberries at every turn.

You would expect the Buddhist religion to turn out a lot of enlightened individuals every year, wouldn't you? I didn't find that to be the case. So what is wrong with this picture? *The more a wave pursues its own wetness as a goal, the further away the wave gets from being its wetness.*

As I mentioned before, the tendency to take up spirituality as a cure for your psychological problems is called "spiritual bypassing." You try to bypass all your problems with the magic bullet of meditation. It sounds good and looks good and actually works to some degree, but without doing the foundational psychological work along the way, nothing much is going to change, in my opinion.

Too many people and meditation teachers in particular, honestly think every problem can be solved with meditation. If you are out of work and depressed, and your guru tells you to meditate more, it is probably time to get another teacher and to find a job.

On the other hand (there is always another "on the other hand" when dealing with paradox), I often see people busying themselves by digging into their childhood traumas in self-help workshops or with their psychiatrist or therapist. Those "archeological digs" can sometimes lead to greater insight into why we do what we do, but far too often, it is simply another expression of narcissism.

I had a client who washed her hands a hundred times a day and knew exactly why she did it, but she still could not stop. I sometimes think some folks would be a lot better off if they spent their day helping people in a homeless shelter instead of incessantly talking about their problems.

The most common expression of narcissistic behavior I see is the incessant striving for enlightenment. The deep reason you don't make much progress even after decades of meditation and self-help workshops is that you are doing it for yourself. When people take the focus off themselves for even a short time, they find their personal problems miraculously dissolving. That's due to their no longer giving little obsessions the energy needed to perpetuate. Try it. Don't think about yourself for an entire day and see what happens.

Let's say that while indulging in narcissistic pursuits, a person accidentally experiences a spiritual awakening. After all, even a blind squirrel will find an acorn occasionally. It is like a wave briefly glimpsing itself as the entirety of the Ocean. You think you have arrived! But then, the memory fades, and you are back identifying with your old familiar ego/wave again – warts and all.

What good is a spiritual awakening if the wave that experienced it is distorted after experiencing itself as the Ocean? This is often what happens. This means the person must continue to work hard on psychological evolution in order to sustain the awakening. Your personal evolution will continue smoothly if you allow it to happen naturally and don't force anything with your obsessive-compulsive tendencies.

This means:

It is more important to be integrated and authentic at whatever stage you find yourself than to hotly pursue enlightenment with a distorted and desperate psyche.

Let's say the experiences of spiritual awakening become more frequent until they are an abiding state. This is to say, there is awareness of the great Oneness/wetness through all levels of consciousness, including the waking, dreaming, and deep-sleep states. In my opinion, this is the true beginning of a spiritual life. There is now an unfailing awareness of the Ocean working through the wave instead of the wave thinking it is doing all the work. Remember, waves get their existence from deep within the Ocean. It was that way before the spiritual awakening and will continue to be so after that experience.

In spite of my opposition to fanatically pursuing enlightenment, I am not opposed to spiritual practices. I actually consider them as necessary as breathing. Just don't do it to get anywhere or to get anything. In other words, just don't overdo it. Be still and learn what the Universe intends for the day instead of what you want. You will also discover that when you take time to clear your mind and emotions, you will be more effective at everything you might be involved with.

When you stop thinking that the wave and the Ocean are separate, the great Oneness is free to express itself as the infinite Ocean, the relative wave, or both, or neither. The important point is that as long as life continues, the physical and psychological challenges will go on – but you will find you will not be as affected by them. Enlightenment will not grow muscles, nor will it get rid of many lifetimes of rage or sadness. What will surely happen is that every moment will become a natural expression of Play.

You have no idea how lucky you are to have been born in such an enlightened age. Only recently have our perspectives broadened to the point where we can entertain the possibility that these experiences might happen to anyone at any time. This breakthrough in understanding allows for the possibility that these experiences are the inherent birthright of everyone.

I suspect that enlightened experiences have happened in the past to many people all over the world, but how they interpreted it, due to their cultural limitations, has caused a lot of trouble down through the ages. Their interpretation and the social context in which they held their experience is what separated the sages from the religious and social tyrants of this world.

For instance, 3,300 years ago in Egypt, a Pharaoh named Akhenaten had an enlightened experience and interpreted it as the Sun God, Aten, coming to him to start a new religion. Two thousand years ago, Saul of Tarsus (before he became St. Paul) had an experience where he believed Jesus came to him in a blinding light. He interpreted this event as a rationale to proselytize Christianity to the degree that modern Christianity might more accurately be called Paulianity.

Other mystical experiences could possibly have been interpreted as the spirit of the jaguar or eagle coming to someone, thereby vastly limiting their experience. Too many people interpreted those experiences as only happening to them. Feeling that they are somehow special, they go out and start a religion or social movement they should have never started.

So thank your lucky stars you were born at this time when our understanding of such things is so much more advanced. Only now, when mystical experience is understood by enough people as the innate birthright of everyone, can you have the freedom to truly

Play without fear of an inquisition or without becoming deluded about how special you are.

The reason enlightenment or unity consciousness is impossible to obtain is because you already are it.

Just be authentic about who you think you are at all stages of your ongoing evolution and keep your heart and mind open to the possibility of a breakthrough to the great Oneness.

Most people are familiar with the possibility of an "aha!" moment. We have all had the experience of trying to remember something. Only when we quit trying to remember it does the memory become clear.

When I was a kid, newspapers had visual puzzles that claimed the face of Abraham Lincoln was hidden in a large pattern of squiggly lines. I would stare at the visual pattern and rotate it many times, trying to find his face – and nothing. When I relaxed and stopped making an effort, it would magically appear. This spontaneous response is the same as the breakthrough to Oneness. The less you struggle and the more you relax, the better are your chances of having one of those mystical moments.

I suggest you plunge into your individual wave or ego until you uncover the strong undercurrents of your mind/wave. Then integrate and transcend it. Continue going deeper into humanity's collective unconscious, which is similar to the powerful undercurrents of the Ocean. Then integrate and transcend it, and don't forget that to transcend something always means to go beyond and include it. Then dive down to the absolute stillness and darkness at the bottom of the Ocean and at the bottom of your being. This realm of pure awareness needs no integration – it will integrate you!

From the perspective of awareness resides the knowing of the completeness of everything. There is nothing that has to be done. All beings are light beings, warts, and all – perfect as they are. The Universe truly is unfolding as it should.

Well now, that ought to keep you busy for another 10,000 lifetimes. I have done my duty as trickster guru, so have at it. I am going to water the plants. You won't see me chasing after my bliss. I let my bliss chase me!

LIFE AND THE UNIVERSE AT PLAY

You now know everything you need to know to be in a constant state of Play. If you still think you are merely a bad-smelling mammal, adrift in an uncaring world where everyone seems to have more goodies than you, here is the rest of the story.

You are not an insignificant creature. You are the Universe perceiving and knowing itself. Without you, the Universe would lack your unique contribution to its self-awareness. You are necessary to the grand scheme of things. You are as much an expression of the great Oneness as everyone else. Where would the Universe be without you? Think of all the experiences you have gathered over the years that the Universe would not have known if you hadn't lived.

Here is my favorite story on this subject, told to me by my Chinese teacher.

A poor, lowly stonecutter labored all day in the hot sun at the foot of a mountain. One day he paused from his dusty, thankless job to watch a magistrate being carried in his carriage to a nearby town. The tired stonecutter watched with envy as the caravan passed by. He wished he had the influence and power of that man. To his surprise, he suddenly became that wealthy person only to discover the magistrate was also sweltering from the heat and wishing he was the Sun.

So the stonecutter became the Sun. As the Sun, he was enjoying his immense power, but soon, a large dark cloud cut off his influence on the Earth. So he decided to be the more powerful cloud. He no sooner became the cloud than a big wind began to blow him apart. He quickly became the wind. He enjoyed blowing everything around but soon came upon an object over which he had no control.

It was a huge mountain, so he became the unmovable mountain. As he was basking in his massiveness, he became aware of an irresistible force that was whittling him away inch by inch. He wondered, "What force in the Universe could be more powerful than I?" He looked down, and there was the lowly stonecutter.

To help you understand your true worth and manage the complexity of your life, I've identified nine precepts of Play. You can copy them on flash cards and carry them around with you. In moments when you are hopelessly identified with your particular body and its distracting limitations, just whip out a card at random and read it. I expect it will speak to your particular situation.

The Nine Precepts of Play

1. Everything is the great Oneness at Play.

2. The One is love: awareness, transcendent, spontaneous, synchronistic, beyond time and space, and all-embracing. It is the Source of everything, and in your essence, you are that Source.

3. The One is also the many: personal, loving, immanent, cause and effect, and evolving. You are also those expressions of the Oneness at Play.

4. To think you are merely a separate wave in the vast Ocean is to miss the deeper reality that you are the entirety of the Ocean, as well as the wave. This awareness is the foundation of Play.

5. It is important to be integrated and authentic at every stage of your unfolding Playfulness. Be physically healthy, mentally inquisitive, and full of love and compassion in your relationships.

6. There are people in every age who Play. Seek them out, be inspired by them, and go beyond them.

7. Everyone has as many lifetimes as they need to perfect themselves, so relax and Play.

8. Life is not a journey to get someplace on the dance floor. It is a joyous, spontaneous, creative participation in Play.

9. Be open and allow the great Oneness to flow through your three bodies (physical, bioelectric, and auric).

THIS IS PLAY!

Epilogue

What do we do to harmonize with the Universal flow? Eventually, I expect to be elected benevolent dictator of this planet and continue my job (more like a hobby) of uniting all of humanity into one loving mass as we evolve toward being an enlightened species. Boy, do I have my work cut out for me. I hear there are now over 7 billion people on Earth – so I could use a little help here!

Do you think becoming enlightened means you can just sit around reeking of wisdom and compassion all day? No way! Or, as the Daoists say: "Wu Wei," which is understood by the sages as, "do things naturally and spontaneously." In sports terms, it is referred to as "being in the zone." Whether you think you are enlightened or not, get out there and spread the love. Work locally and globally in any way you can to contribute to the natural flow of our evolving toward unity consciousness, which includes everything and is what you already are.

The best way to help is through example, of course. So, what does a good example of wholeness look like? Are you firmly grounded in your body? How is your health? Do you have good eating and sleeping habits? Do you breathe deep into your belly in all circumstances? Do you move with fluidity, grace, and coordination?

How is your chi flowing these days? Do you have abundant energy for whatever you want to do? How is your cellular communication? Do your immune and emotional systems respond appropriately to every situation? If you are allergic to everything that blows in the air, your immune system is excessively aggressive. Your mind should be calm and clear. Are your relationships deep, harmonious, and mutually supportive?

Have you checked out your aura recently? Are all nine vortices bright and in sync with each other? Are you free to come and go from your body? Have you met any interesting, high-frequency intergalactic beings lately? (Knowing me doesn't count.) If you were able to answer a resounding "yes" to all of the above, you qualify to join our Daoist Immortals Club, which has recently grown by one. There is plenty of room for more members, and we have many long-lasting benefits. I look forward to adding you to our club.

A final thought:

Since I mentioned that everything started with the Big Bang, I would like to end with my understanding of what everything is evolving toward. Although the Universe is still expanding, and much faster than expected, I subscribe to the theory that there will come a time when the gravity among all the billions of galaxies will overpower the expansion, and it will start to contract – as it may have done countless times before.

The merging of our Milky Way galaxy with Andromeda, referred to earlier, is only one of the billions of galactic mergers to come. These will create a super gravitational mass that will collapse into itself. Eventually, all the available gas will be used up, and all the stars that converted that gas to light will burn out. There will only be darkness unto the deep. That gigantic dark mass of burned-out stars and black holes will compress until the density and heat become so enormous, it will explode into another Universe, and off we go again – another Universe in the endless procession of those that have come before and those that will follow. So, you see, our Universe is finite in its expansion AND infinite in its continuous cycles of creation and dissolution – just like us!

From this deep awareness, there is the knowing that everything is already complete. There is nothing that has to be done. All beings are light beings – perfect as they are. The Universe truly is unfolding as it should.

If you have been wondering what Mark is up to these days, he is enthusiastically promoting his book while in exile for his outrageous statements.

About the Author

Mark Johnson is a semi-retired Tai Ji and Chi Gung instructor and healer. He continues to judge Tai Ji tournaments regularly, serves on the Advisory Council to the National Qigong Association, and leads Daoist retreats to China and Tibet yearly.

He sells his Tai Chi for Seniors video and other instructional DVDs through his online company: *TaiChiForSeniorsVideo.com* (800,000 sales so far!).

Mark has studied and practiced Eastern Philosophy for more than 50 years and has apprenticed with some of the world's most prominent Vedanta, Zen, and Daoist teachers.

For nearly 15 years, he has been a member and research subject of the Institute of Noetic Sciences. He lives in Northern California, where he engages in amateur astronomy and enjoys flying his ultralight aircraft. Most importantly, he is the proud father of his grown daughter, Sita.

Made in the USA
Monee, IL
25 January 2021